A LETTER FROM PETER MUNK

Since we started the Munk Debates, my wife, Melanie, and I have been deeply gratified at how quickly they have captured the public's imagination. From the time of our first event in May 2008, we have hosted what I believe are some of the most exciting public policy debates in Canada and internationally. Global in focus, the Munk Debates have tackled a range of issues, such as humanitarian intervention, the effectiveness of foreign aid, the threat of global warming, religion's impact on geopolitics, the rise of China, and the decline of Europe. These compelling topics have served as intellectual and ethical grist for some of the world's most important thinkers and doers, from Henry Kissinger to Tony Blair, Christopher Hitchens to Paul Krugman, Peter Mandelson to Fareed Zakaria.

The issues raised at the Munk Debates have not only fostered public awareness, but they have also helped many of us become more involved and, therefore, less intimidated by the concept of globalization. It is so easy to be inward-looking. It is so easy to be xenophobic. It is so easy to be nationalistic. It is hard to go into the unknown. Globalization, for many people, is an abstract concept at best. The purpose of this debate series is to help people feel more familiar with our fast-changing world and more comfortable participating in the universal dialogue about the issues and events that will shape our collective future.

I don't need to tell you that that there are many, many burning issues. Global warming, the plight of extreme poverty, genocide, our shaky financial order: these are just a few of the critical issues that matter to people. And it seems to me, and to my foundation board members, that the quality of the public dialogue on these critical issues diminishes in direct proportion to the salience and number of these issues clamouring for our attention. By trying to highlight the most important issues at crucial moments in the global conversation, these debates not only profile the ideas and opinions of some of the world's brightest thinkers, but they also crystallize public passion and knowledge, helping to tackle some of the challenges confronting humankind.

I have learned in life—and I'm sure many of you will share this view—that challenges bring out the best in us. I hope you'll agree that the participants in these debates challenge not only each other but also each of us to think clearly and logically about important problems facing our world.

Peter Munk
Founder, Aurea Foundation
Toronto, Ontario

IS AMERICAN DEMOCRACY IN CRISIS?

DIONNE AND SULLIVAN VS. GINGRICH AND STRASSEL

THE MUNK DEBATES

Edited by Rudyard Griffiths

ANANSI

This edition published in 2018 by
House of Anansi Press Inc.
www.houseofanansi.com

House of Anansi Press is committed to protecting our natural environment. As part of our efforts, the interior of this book is printed on paper that contains 100% post-consumer recycled fibres, is acid-free, and is processed chlorine-free.

22 21 20 19 18   1 2 3 4 5

Library and Archives Canada Cataloguing in Publication

Is American democracy in crisis? : Dionne and Sullivan
vs. Gingrich and Strassel / edited by Rudyard Griffiths.

(The Munk debates)
Issued in print and electronic formats.
ISBN 978-1-4870-0451-4 (softcover).—ISBN 978-1-4870-0452-1
(EPUB).—ISBN 978-1-4870-0453-8 (Kindle)

1. Democracy—United States. 2. United States—Politics and government—2017-. I. Gingrich, Newt panelist II. Sullivan, Andrew, 1963- panelist III. Griffiths, Rudyard, editor IV. Strassel, Kimberley A panelist V. Dionne, E. J., Jr panelist VI. Series: Munk debates

JK1726.I8 2018   320.473   C2017-907407-5
                        C2017-907408-3

Library of Congress Control Number: 2017961328

Cover design: Alysia Shewchuk
Text design and typesetting: Sara Loos
Transcription: Transcript Heroes

Canada Council   Conseil des Arts
for the Arts   du Canada

ONTARIO ARTS COUNCIL
CONSEIL DES ARTS DE L'ONTARIO
an Ontario government agency
un organisme du gouvernement de l'Ontario

We acknowledge for their financial support of our publishing program the Canada Council for the Arts, the Ontario Arts Council, and the Government of Canada through the Canada Book Fund.

Printed and bound in Canada

CONTENTS

Pre-Debate Interviews with Moderator
Rudyard Griffiths

NEWT GINGRICH IN CONVERSATION
WITH RUDYARD GRIFFITHS

RUDYARD GRIFFITHS: Joining me to share his thoughts on the current state of American democracy is former Speaker of the United States House of Representatives Newt Gingrich. It's a real pleasure to host you here in Toronto for your third Munk Debate.

NEWT GINGRICH: It's great to be back with you.

RUDYARD GRIFFITHS: Let's get your views on the state of American democracy today. Do you acknowledge that there is a crisis underway?

NEWT GINGRICH: I think there is a very profound shaking of the system — on both the Right and the Left. I think part of it is something we're seeing happen all over the world, in the elections in Catalonia, Austria, Britain, and

Germany. There is a pattern right now of people being unhappy, people wanting a level of change, people feeling that government is failing them and that their leadership is failing them.

America is part of a worldwide phenomenon. Part of it is that there has been a mutation of the American Left into a remarkably hostile and in many ways racist system in which you have a repudiation of the very concept of America. And on the right you have a smaller but strong movement that is also anti-politician and against the system at large. So you have, on both extremes, forces that are deeply hostile to the existing system and that are, I think, going to cause a very substantial conflict over the next ten or twenty years.

RUDYARD GRIFFITHS: Your opponents tonight are going to try to push the case that Donald Trump is an accelerant of these tensions that are tearing at the fabric of American society. His comments on race, on American culture, on American nationalism — they are going to portray these as exceedingly negative, exceedingly divisive, fuelling this so-called crisis. What's your push-back?

NEWT GINGRICH: Well, I'm not sure I'm going to push back. I'm prepared to say that Trump is the great clarifier; he describes what already exists. He didn't invent the fight over the National Football League — people taking a knee or in some way repudiating the American flag and the national anthem. What he did was clarify that for two-thirds of all Americans that was unacceptable behaviour.

In the case of Charlottesville, he described that there was violence on both sides, and he got attacked for it. That's objectively true. I mean, you have Antifa, a movement which believes in violence. And at the College of William & Mary the other day, the American Civil Liberties Union (ACLU) spokesperson was shouted down and surrounded by Black Lives Matter protestors, who said she shouldn't be allowed to speak on the campus. You have people who are consistently on the left advocating a variety of things that are horrendous and that represent the end of the American system as we know it.

Trump's role in all that is to take those people head-on, to cut through the political correctness, and to arouse the majority of Americans to say this is wrong.

RUDYARD GRIFFITHS: You're a master legislator, someone with an immense amount of experience getting things through a complicated congressional system in the United States. Months into this administration, not a single significant piece of legislation has been passed. Is that a crisis that is debatable tonight?

NEWT GINGRICH: It's not a crisis, but it's a problem. They have a real challenge in the next few weeks to pass the tax cut. I think it is the most important single thing in this first two years. I think if they pass the tax cut and the economy booms, the Republicans will do very well in 2018. I think if they can't get this tax cut passed, they have very deep problems and they are going to have a very bad election next year.

RUDYARD GRIFFITHS: And how about some of the other major planks of this president's agenda? Key promises to his voting constituency, a so-called wall across the southern U.S. border with Mexico? It doesn't seem any closer today than—

NEWT GINGRICH: Well, it's going well. It's much closer. They have hundreds of miles that have already been completed. Some of them are virtual walls that are electronic. Some of them are metal rather than concrete.

Illegal crossing on the southern border is down, I think, 78 percent. That's a pretty remarkable achievement. And they have clearly signalled that they are going to be much tougher on illegal immigration, and I think that that's what most Americans want. I think most Americans think that we're very much for legal immigration but we're very much opposed to illegal immigration.

RUDYARD GRIFFITHS: We got roughly 25,000 comments on Facebook in the lead-up to tonight's debate. It's really something out of the ordinary.

NEWT GINGRICH: Is that a record for the Munk Debates?

RUDYARD GRIFFITHS: It is, absolutely. I think it shows the intensity of passions around this subject, the state of American democracy. One of the lines coming out of those comments that recurs again and again from supporters of President Trump is that they believe the crisis of American democracy lies with the Obama administration and with the Clinton camp within the Democratic Party. Do you subscribe to that argument?

NEWT GINGRICH: I certainly think that President Obama had a remarkable opportunity to unify the country and instead he divided it. His reaction to Ferguson was so anti-police; his reactions again and again were in many cases factually wrong and divisive. I think his failure to even try to fix the inner cities is so painful.

The number of people who were shot in Chicago in his eight-year presidency is just breathtaking. The total failure of the Baltimore school system to save young African Americans in poor neighbourhoods is so stunning. And he did nothing to try to help the very poor or to unify the country.

But I think Obama was a symptom of a much deeper problem. College professors under thirty-five are 12:1 Democrat. What you now have is an emergence of a very left-wing academic world, surrounded by a very left-wing news media with a very left-wing Hollywood, and the three reinforce each other. And with people like George Soros putting the money in, you have the emergence of a nationwide network of very aggressive, very hostile left-wing activists. Those are all factors that are dividing the country. And as a part of that process you have millions of Americans who react and say that they don't agree with what they are doing. And I think that's going to become much more intense.

There is a whole cycle building now. I just looked at a study of Edina, which is a school system in Minnesota that has historically been a very good system, one of the best in Minnesota. It was taken over by left-wingers who decided that their job wasn't to teach kids, it was to sensitize them. And so, they now have a very left-wing, racist agenda in which they spend most of their energy trying to convince white kids that they should be inferior and they should feel guilt-ridden, et cetera. And the result is that they have had a twenty-five or thirty point drop in the school scores. I mean, they are no longer teaching.

That's happening all across the country. That's going to lead to a reaction by people who think that children ought to learn how to read and write and get a job and be functional. So, in that sense we really are more polarized than we have been at any point since the Vietnam War.

RUDYARD GRIFFITHS: We've talked about the cultural and political dimensions of the so-called crisis of American democracy. I want to end on the economic dimension. Some people have accused this president and advisers like Steve Bannon of racializing economic grievances and pushing a political message that pits Americans against each other based on their racial identity. What's your reply to that argument?

NEWT GINGRICH: Well, my sense is Trump stands for economic growth for everybody. He stands for jobs for everybody. He's adamantly in favour of legal immigration. He's married to an immigrant. His mother was an immigrant. But he's also deeply opposed to illegal immigration. I don't think being opposed to illegal immigration is racist. It's the rule of law.

The tax cuts are going to apply to everybody. Whether you're an African American or a Latino or an Asian small business owner, you are going to get the same tax break as a white small business owner. So, in that sense I think it's a pretty big stretch to argue that there is a racial component of his economic policy.

RUDYARD GRIFFITHS: Finally, I want to touch on your insight and professional training as a historian. What moment in America's past do you think best captures where the United States is today? A moment ago, you mentioned Vietnam. Are there other chapters of American history that you think illuminate the present and maybe tell us what the future could look like?

NEWT GINGRICH: There are three very different moments that might throw some light on where we are now. One is the rise of Andrew Jackson, the first real populist to break through, and the most disruptive person to be president prior to Trump. There are a lot of similarities between Jackson and Trump in personality, in disruption, and in the hostility of the establishment. I always tell people if you are going to drain the swamp you should assume the alligators will be really mad. And that's part of what's going on here.

Second, I think, is Lincoln. If you look at Trump's inaugural address and then you look at the mass rallies the next day — Madonna saying she dreams of the White

9

House being destroyed, et cetera—the reaction was very much like Lincoln's first inaugural. There are real patterns, in fact, between how Trump approached his campaign and his election and how Lincoln approached his inaugural. And, it turns out, there are real patterns between how Southern slavery newspapers attacked Lincoln and how the Left has attacked Trump. It's a very weird parallel.

And then, third, is Theodore Roosevelt. Roosevelt was very popular, but he was astonishingly energetic and he broke out of the norms and kept the establishment constantly off-balance. I have always told people if you took Jackson for disruption and Roosevelt for energy and P. T. Barnum for salesmanship, somewhere in those three you have got Donald Trump.

RUDYARD GRIFFITHS: Newt Gingrich, thank you for your time today.

NEWT GINGRICH: Thank you.

KIMBERLEY STRASSEL IN CONVERSATION
WITH RUDYARD GRIFFITHS

RUDYARD GRIFFITHS: Joining me now is Kimberley Strassel, a columnist with the *Wall Street Journal* who will be arguing alongside Newt Gingrich against the motion: "Be it resolved, American democracy is in its worst crisis in a generation and Donald J. Trump is to blame." Kimberley, great to have you here in Toronto.

KIMBERLEY STRASSEL: It's great to be here.

RUDYARD GRIFFITHS: Give me your sense of where American democracy is at this moment. Do you buy into the notion that there is a crisis?

KIMBERLEY STRASSEL: There is no question that there is a lot of controversy and upheaval in the United States, that we're probably more divided now than we've been in a while, and that the president feeds a lot of this. And if that's the argument, then you could say things are a bit dire.

But in the United States we have documents that define what democracy actually is — government by the people for the people — and that outline a separation of powers and the rights of individuals. And on that level, I would argue Donald Trump has done more to help get us back to a place of real democracy.

RUDYARD GRIFFITHS: Can you give us some examples?

KIMBERLEY STRASSEL: Well, his predecessor, Barack Obama, came to office with an agenda and acknowledged that it needed to be passed through Congress. But when Congress wouldn't pass it, he just decided to issue it by edict from the Oval Office. There was a lot of concern about this. I don't know how much it filtered up to Canada, but a lot of the backlash that fuelled the anger and elected Donald Trump was people feeling that there was a lawless government in Washington.

For instance, Barack Obama's climate change program was supposed to be done by statute through Congress. Instead, he just enacted it by regulation. Or take the immigration question, the Young American Dreamers — I'm a passionate believer in allowing them to stay in the United States, by the way, but you don't just get to do it with the stroke of the pen. He acknowledged this was something Congress was supposed to do and then later just forgot about all that.

RUDYARD GRIFFITHS: You played a very active role in the Trump campaign, covering it for the *Wall Street Journal*. Trump's critics have said that it fundamentally was an unsound election, that there were factors at play: Russia, the news media and its treatment of Trump. How do you respond?

KIMBERLEY STRASSEL: The complaints were on both sides. There was a big complaint among Republicans that the media did not treat Donald Trump fairly in the run-up to the campaign. You could also argue that just by virtue of him being who he was, he got a lot of free air time on TV. So, I think that's almost a draw in terms of a fight.

The Russia stuff — it's important that people realize that to this day there has not been any evidence that there was collusion between the Trump team and Russia. We do know that the Russians were trying to interfere in our election, but we've had reassurances from every major state official and federal official that that did not affect a vote tally.

So, I think that this is a little bit of sour grapes after the fact. There is also frustration, I know, among many on the left and critics of Donald Trump about our electoral college system. But it's what the framers set out. That's how we've elected presidents since the beginning. It would take two-thirds of the states to change that, or actually more, and that's just not going to happen for a long time.

RUDYARD GRIFFITHS: How do you feel, though, about the state of this president's legitimacy in the face of, let's say, not releasing his tax returns, a simple tradition that all previous candidates had engaged in. Not being more forthcoming about his own current business relationships vis-à-vis the Trump Organization. Are those features of a self-made crisis that this president has to share some blame for?

KIMBERLEY STRASSEL: Everyone shares blame in this, and he does, first and foremost. He should have released his taxes. And he also should have divested himself of most of his businesses, just to get rid of that hanging over him. He should be more careful in what he tweets and what he says. I know that some of his base supporters adore his raw honesty, but he ends up getting into fights that only hurt him and don't necessarily help the aims of the things that he wants in office.

That being said, I think that the crisis of legitimacy of this president has also been caused by an American media that has lost its traditional sense of fair coverage. They view themselves now as attack dogs because they personally dislike this president, and that is a problem.

We also have a lot of things to get into, to get to the bottom of. In terms of this Russia discussion, there is not a lot of evidence out there that the Russians were involved in some of these allegations that have so hit this presidency. And, if this was a disinformation campaign on their behalf, they have done a very good job of it.

RUDYARD GRIFFITHS: Indeed. Lots to unpack there, and I'm sure it will be a feature of tonight's debate. Let's switch to topics associated with culture, because critics of this president have said that he has abandoned a more inclusive, broader view of American patriotism, of American nationalism, and American identity to focus instead on a base that's predominantly white, predominantly working class, and predominantly shares views that are antithetical maybe to immigrants, to the LGBTQ community. To what extent does the president have a responsibility to rise above those divisions and act as a unifier and not a divider?

KIMBERLEY STRASSEL: We want our presidents to be unifiers because one thing that is particularly unique about the United States presidency is once you step into that Oval Office you take a pledge to defend all Americans. You are America's president. And the goal, which has been the case with many presidents in the past, is to set aside your partisan politics.

I think Barack Obama broke that mould first in that he was a very partisan president. Just in terms of being very demeaning about Republicans and his opponents and very much leaving you to feel that if you were not part of his party then he really didn't consider you part of the forward motion of the United States.

Donald Trump has taken that to new levels. And it's unfortunate for him and for the Republican Party, because we know from history that the political leaders who do the best are those who are inclusive—those who invite and persuade more people to join their cause. And tweets at 2:00 a.m. that are 140 characters long are not a very good way of persuading people.

Now, we have seen this president change tack a little since John Kelly became chief of staff. And I would note, for instance, the very big distinction between how he handled the health care debate, in which he left the Republicans on their own and even skewered them for not moving faster or doing what he wanted, and this time, where he is actually on a road show across the United States, making the case for tax reform. That's how you get people on your side, and we can only hope that's something he replicates in the years to come.

RUDYARD GRIFFITHS: What moment in America's past do you think most accurately captures the mood of the country today?

KIMBERLEY STRASSEL: I think we all have to be careful. Humanity has a way of always thinking pityingly, that we are in the worst situation ever. And, of course, there are many times in the history of the United States and the world that have been far worse than Donald Trump.

From a very broad sense, Donald Trump defies a lot of historical periods. He is no *one* politician. He is an odd mix of a lot of different things. He is not even necessarily, as most people understand the term, a real Republican.

But I think if you went back, what best fits the mood of the country today is the populism of the Jacksonian era. That is why Donald Trump is in office. There is a class of Americans out there that feel that they have been forgotten, and Trump has tapped into that. The challenge for Donald Trump is to make the distinction between policies that are good for the future of the United States and those that are temporarily popular with a small group of Americans that are his most ardent supporters.

RUDYARD GRIFFITHS: Kimberley, we are going to leave it there. Thanks.

KIMBERLEY STRASSEL: Thank you.

E. J. DIONNE IN CONVERSATION
WITH RUDYARD GRIFFITHS

RUDYARD GRIFFITHS: E. J. Dionne is a *Washington Post* columnist and the co-author of a great new book, *One Nation After Trump: A Guide for the Perplexed, the Disheartened, the Desperate, and the Not-Yet Deported.* Let's dive right in here, because I think one of the central arguments you are going to face in this debate is the notion that the crisis of American democracy predates Trump. Trump is simply a symptom; he is not a cause.

E. J. DIONNE: Well, I think the fact that the other side of this debate is going to go there, to that part of the resolution, suggests how weak the case for Donald Trump actually is. And, obviously, if it goes there, that's part of what we're going to be arguing. History goes on; it doesn't begin. You can't turn on a switch and say history starts now.

So, if someone wants to argue that we had many problems in America before Donald Trump was there, that's clearly the case. The question is, did we face a crisis of the sort we face right now? And I don't think we did. We certainly didn't face a crisis of this sort under President Obama. We faced a lot of deep problems and divisions under President Bush, but I don't think we have been at a point before in the history of the United States where Americans are really worried about whether the leader of their country is an autocrat.

I arrived here the day after President Trump said that he wants to pull the licence of NBC News. Now, the first problem with that statement is there is no licence for a network in the United States, so it's a factual error. But, more importantly, a president of the United States threatening a television network because he doesn't like what it reports?

The same day, President Trump said that there is something wrong with people saying whatever it is they want. And I thought that was the definition of free speech. So, does President Trump want to repeal the First Amendment?

I think what we are dealing with in Trump is someone who has taken a series of problems we faced before — there is no question — but pushed us far beyond where we were into a point of genuine crisis.

RUDYARD GRIFFITHS: I want to go further with you on the theme of autocracy, because it's a big part of *One Nation After Trump*. What are the elements that would allow you, a scholar of political science, society, and culture, to say that this isn't just bravado, this isn't just someone sounding off, but that there is a real danger here — that there is an autocratic sentiment that is shared more broadly by the president and perhaps by a lot of your fellow Americans who voted for him?

E. J. DIONNE: I think that there are some who voted for him who may share that sentiment. I think there are others who voted for him because they were mad about various things. And I won't begin to try to understand Donald Trump's psychology and exactly why he says these things. I just judge him by what he says. I can't recall an American politician who went before a national convention of his or her party and said, "I alone can fix it." I don't think we've had, in the same way, a president who attacks the courts, attacks the media, demonizes his opponents beyond just the normal give-and-take of politics, but really tries to suggest that his opposition is illegitimate.

And those are the marks of people who have slowly chipped away at democracy in other countries — whether you are looking at Erdoğan in Turkey, Putin in Russia, or Orbán in Hungary. We're not there yet. And I don't have to worry when I go back to the United States — I hope — about being arrested or not being let in when I land at Dulles Airport tomorrow. But I do worry very much about a leader who has these ideas in his head and who somehow seems to have no respect for the norms, customs, or traditions of the office that he holds, and no real sense of the responsibility that that involves, and very little sense of what the words "republicanism" or "democracy" actually mean.

RUDYARD GRIFFITHS: Let me try out another argument that I think you are going to hear from your opponents: the Left and the progressive movement in the United States has engaged in a form of identity politics that is driving the country apart. It is creating a series of divisions that have festered and now exploded into this crisis. They assign that blame to the progressive Left, which you're a proud member of, and to the Democratic Party, and particularly to the campaign of Hillary Clinton and the issues that she advanced.

E. J. DIONNE: If an African American's unarmed son is shot in the street by the police, and that parent is angry and upset, is that identity politics or is that simply a call for justice? If women are discriminated against in the workplace and say this is wrong, is that identity politics or a call for justice? If Latinos are worried about the discrimination they face, is that identity politics or a call for justice?

I think that some of the supporters of President Trump, probably including our sparring partners tonight, are trying to argue that anybody who stands up for the rights of any minority is engaged in identity politics. What are you supposed to do if you are a progressive? Are you supposed to say, Well, I am not going to speak up for that woman or that African American or that Latino because, God forbid, Newt Gingrich or someone else will accuse me of identity politics?

Now, if somebody wants to argue that there are many aspects of identity politics that relate to class — which in a way is also its own form of identity politics — I certainly believe that. Our country's slogan, *E pluribus unum* (Out of many, one), acknowledges the many. It also says that we are one nation. And I think the liberal or progressive project is to defend the rights of particular groups who face particular forms of oppression and discrimination, but also to assert that we have a shared national interest, and that many of the problems faced by African Americans in the inner city, for example, are quite similar economically to those faced in predominantly white middle-class towns like Reading or Erie, Pennsylvania.

I think those who cry identity politics are really trying to hold the pain of one group, in this case the white working class, against the pain of another group, African Americans or Latinos. That kind of politics is a recipe for division and inaction.

RUDYARD GRIFFITHS: Turning to the economic dimension of this crisis, some people have charged that this president is racializing economic grievances in America to disastrous effect. Do you believe that that is a major feature of the democratic crisis that America confronts?

E. J. DIONNE: I think that, unfortunately, President Trump has racialized issues for a long time. You can go back to his and his father's company facing charges of discrimination. You can go back to birtherism — the belief that Barack Obama was really born in Kenya, not in the

23

United States — which was clearly redolent with racial themes.

There is a long tradition in the United States of trying to split the discontented by using racial politics. The old populist movement in the South was split by the exploitation of a racial division. And I do think it's very important for progressives to bring together the cause of racial justice with the cause of economic justice.

I have been thinking a lot lately about the great 1963 March on Washington, where Martin Luther King gave his "I Have a Dream" speech. The slogan of that march was "Jobs and Freedom." And what that slogan, I think, embodies is this idea that you can't separate racial justice from economic justice, and you can't separate economic justice from racial justice. The job of progressives is to fight efforts to divide people along those lines.

RUDYARD GRIFFITHS: I want to end by asking you to reach back into your understanding of American history and politics to give us a sense of what moment in America's past you think correlates to where the country is today, and does that moment provide us with any clues for where America is headed in terms of this intense moment of division?

E. J. DIONNE: I am hopeful that it can be overcome. I'll start there partly by looking at the attitudes of Americans under the age of forty-five. There is a very different kind of politics going on among younger Americans on many of these issues. And I think it would be unnatural for us to stay this divided for a lengthy period.

On the other hand, I am very alarmed by what we face right now. I forget who said it first, but it's a bit like we are in a cold civil war. Not a civil war with guns and bullets — for the most part, thank God — but a depth of division that is almost as profound as that of a civil war, because the divisions are cultural, ideological, and by age, region, and race. There are a lot of reinforcing forms of division.

The time that I have been thinking about a lot is the period of the 1850s. And we know that the 1850s ended in a real civil war. My prayer is that we won't get there. I think we can avoid that. And I would point to the fact that the country as a whole, if you judge by all of the polling, has largely rejected Trump and Trumpism. His approval rating has been in the thirties, up to maybe 40 percent. A substantial majority of Americans reject this kind of politics and want something less divisive and more unifying.

So, I think it's not simply my tendency sometimes to be a glass one-tenth-full person, and to hope that there is something better out there than seems to be going on. I really do think that we will overcome this. But I do worry also about the damage that could be caused over the next four years.

RUDYARD GRIFFITHS: E. J. Dionne, terrific analysis, terrific insights.

E. J. DIONNE: Thank you.

ANDREW SULLIVAN IN CONVERSATION
WITH RUDYARD GRIFFITHS

RUDYARD GRIFFITHS: Joining me now for his views on the debate and on the state of American democracy is political commentator and author Andrew Sullivan. Andrew, great to have you as part of this group tonight.

ANDREW SULLIVAN: Great to be here.

RUDYARD GRIFFITHS: I want to kick off by having you encapsulate for us a terrific essay that you wrote on tribalism in America. Why do you think tribal instinct is key to understanding the real challenges facing American democracy today?

ANDREW SULLIVAN: Well, it helps explain how rationality has kind of disappeared—how the normal functioning of democracy, which requires the assessment of arguments, the rebuttal of ideas, the engagement between one particular position and another, has kind of collapsed into these two tribes, the red tribe and the blue tribe, who are fundamentally motivated by feeling, not argument, and are disturbingly also overlapping in terms of region, in terms of race, and in terms of religion, which are three factors that define tribally-fractured societies. And I see this getting entrenched. I see this as the thought of both sides, although I do think that the Republican Party bears the bulk of the blame in this, or at least has an edge. Moreover, Donald Trump, in his campaign and in his so far disastrous presidency, has only exacerbated, intentionally intensified, and exploited this division to sustain himself politically.

RUDYARD GRIFFITHS: We have had an incredible reaction on social media to this debate, over 25,000 comments on our main page. And I think that reaction speaks to the intensity of these tribes, who have very different views on this president. One of the consistent themes that comes out of the comments on our Facebook page from supporters of this president is a very deeply held belief that the divisions, the crisis of American democracy, resides with the previous administration — that there was something in Barack Obama's presidency that, from their own subjective experience, made many Americans feel that America was no longer a place they could call home. What are your thoughts on that sentiment?

ANDREW SULLIVAN: A place to call home? America is home to anybody who has citizenship, and I think should be home to anybody who travels there and who loves the place. I'm an immigrant to America. I'm now an American citizen and for me it is home. And I utterly sympathize with people who are beset by forces that are bewildering them — forces of mass immigration that they feel have changed the culture and nature of their society; the onslaught of free trade, which has clearly punished some sectors of the economy and of society more than others; automation and technology, which has cut them off at the knees, in some respects; and increasing secularization, which has made many Christians feel besieged, to some extent.

I understand all that. But Barack Obama was a man who deliberately ran to be president of both red and blue America, who ran saying there are no red states and blue states, just the United States of America, and who pursued what I take to be a completely mainstream, rather moderate position with a temperament and a rhetoric that was always mollifying and moderate.

I don't understand why people responded the way they did, unless it is some function of the fact that he's called Barack Hussein Obama and is the first biracial president of the United States. And that might be one thing. But then to turn to someone so manifestly unfit, so psychologically unstable, so temperamentally autocratic, so fathomlessly ignorant, and so constantly mendacious, is to act irresponsibly toward their own home.

RUDYARD GRIFFITHS: Good point. Another argument that we're probably going to hear tonight from your opponents is that there is a segment of American society who have, in their view, been cast off by a Washington elite who is self-dealing and self-interested. As one of our commenters on Facebook put it: "I voted for Donald Trump because he is my murder weapon." Basically, there was an idea here that this president would be the disrupter-in-chief. They probably couldn't care less if he is going to be one of America's great presidents by the verdict or judgement of history.

ANDREW SULLIVAN: That's a despicable view to take. It's a reckless, irresponsible view to take. You don't elect a president to be a murder weapon, whatever that means. And why would you want to murder your fellow citizens? They have plenty of flaws. They should be robustly criticized. They have failed. They failed militarily. They failed economically. They failed in terms of their ability to be in a bubble, free of the stresses of many other people, and not seeing their own blindness. All of which you can concede.

But to respond in this irrational way, to elect someone so clearly incapable of doing the job, who is also simultaneously a threat to the democratic constitutional order; who despises a free press; who tells lies every day of the week; whose own secretary of state has called him a f-ing moron; who the Republican chairman of the Senate Committee on Foreign Relations has said requires an adult daycare centre to keep under control and is risking World War III — do you think that's a patriotic thing to do? It is a despicable thing to do. It is an unforgiveable thing to do.

It may be understandable emotionally, but we're a democracy. We do not let our irrational feelings completely swamp our minds and our frontal cortexes. If you believe in this country and its Constitution, those very procedures and norms and institutions that have protected our freedoms for so long, then you should defend them rather than elect someone who is essentially a vandal, wrecking America from within.

This man is a threat to you and to me, to America, a country I love, and to the security of everyone in it and around the world. He is someone who can play with the idea that he could initiate a war that would kill hundreds of thousands of people, someone who celebrates torture, someone who tells police officers to manhandle their suspects, someone who is threatening the licence of a television station because it dares broadcast the truth about him. This is a monster who should be cast out of the office as soon as possible, preferably by the Twenty-fifth Amendment.

RUDYARD GRIFFITHS: Hearing you now, I feel that you believe this isn't simply a passing crisis, comparable perhaps to the presidency of Richard Nixon. Do you think that there is something greater at stake here? A greater set of moral collective perils that face Americans with this presidency?

ANDREW SULLIVAN: It's a state of emergency. We've been in a state of emergency since January 20, 2017. We have a president incapable of understanding reality. We have a president who is utterly irrational. We have a president who cannot control himself, who is in control of all of us.

And it wasn't until the end of his term that Nixon, who also was a threat to American democracy, began to act in these disgusting and irrational ways. Trump has begun this way.

Not only that, Trump intends to destroy what he inherited. He has no interest in protecting and preserving the institutions and Constitution of the United States, and has declared so every day. The threat he poses, also in a way that Nixon didn't, is to the very fabric of our society: the way he will never lose an opportunity to exploit race and divisions within the country to elevate himself; the pathological narcissism with which he cannot concern himself with any other interests than his own; the way he uses the presidency of the United States to attack individual citizens, smearing them, lying about them. This is a man who lies and refuses ever to retract any of the lies he has told. The *Washington Post* has now tallied 1,300 separate absolute falsehoods this man has spoken in office. He is a man who regards the presidency as something that does not require even the most minimal form of responsibility. If he had been made the CEO of a publicly traded company on January 20, he would have been removed by the board on January 21. And yet he sits there.

Everybody in Washington knows this. Did you see many Republican senators standing up to attack Senator Corker? No. They know.

But he is also—in a way that Nixon never was, in a way that no president in my lifetime or before has ever been— a demagogue, someone who is willing to use the mob to whip up passions to enforce his will. He's a threat in that sense; he's a uniquely populist demagogue, certainly fascistic in his practices, if not in his actual policies, and therefore a danger to us all.

RUDYARD GRIFFITHS: Let me end with a question that I have asked all of our debaters. Is there a moment in America's past that you think corresponds to the mood and the state of the country today? And if there is, what does that moment tell us about where America could be headed?

ANDREW SULLIVAN: I think you could look to the early 1860s or the mid-1960s, when the country was so implacably divided against itself that it had ceased to be a country at all.

The truth is that the two tribes in America hate each other more than they love their country. They hate each other more than they loathe any other country on earth. And they are now prepared, certainly on the right, to destroy the core institutions of their country out of sheer anger and rage and bigotry. They are better than that. They know they are better than that. We are all better than that. We are all better than the president who is destroying the fabric of the democracy he is supposed to uphold.

I don't regard this debate as an esoteric exercise. There is a huge amount at stake in America. And every day that goes by without a catastrophe is a miracle. But every day, Trump's poison further makes the atmosphere in America toxic.

RUDYARD GRIFFITHS: Thanks again, Andrew.

Is American Democracy in Crisis?

Pro: E. J. Dionne Jr. and Andrew Sullivan
Con: Newt Gingrich and Kimberley Strassel

October 12, 2017
Toronto, Ontario

RUDYARD GRIFFITHS: Good evening, ladies and gentlemen. I want to welcome the Canada-wide audience tuning in to this debate right now on CBC and CPAC, and across the continental United States on C-SPAN.

A warm hello also to our online audience watching this debate on Facebook Live, our exclusive social media partner, and on Bloomberg.com. It's great to have you as virtual participants in tonight's proceedings.

And hello to you, the over 3,000 people who have filled Roy Thomson Hall for yet another Munk Debate. We salute your interest, your commitment, and your desire for informed public discussion of the big issues of the day.

I want to take this opportunity to acknowledge that our ability year-in and year-out, debate-in and debate-out, to bring some of the world's sharpest minds and brightest thinkers to this stage, to the city of Toronto, to debate these big issues that are on our minds, that have captured our attention, would not be possible without the public-spiritedness and the generosity of our hosts tonight. Ladies and gentlemen, Peter and Melanie Munk. Bravo, you two.

Well, we are just moments from getting our two teams out here on centre stage where they will be tackling tonight's resolution, one that's on all our minds: "Be it resolved, American democracy is in its worst crisis in a generation and Donald J. Trump is to blame."

Arguing in favour of the resolution is the renowned editor, father of the modern-day blog, and celebrated social commentator—ladies and gentlemen, Andrew Sullivan.

Andrew's debating partner tonight is the bestselling author of numerous books, a scholar at the prestigious Brookings Institution, and a must-read columnist at the *Washington Post*. Ladies and gentlemen, E. J. Dionne.

Now, one team of great debaters deserves another. So, let's welcome back to the stage a formidable debater, the former Speaker of the U.S. House of Representatives and the author of the recent bestselling book *Understanding Trump*. Ladies and gentlemen, Newt Gingrich.

Our final debater tonight, Newt Gingrich's teammate, is a celebrated *Wall Street Journal* columnist and well-known U.S. political commentator. Ladies and gentlemen, Kimberley Strassel.

Now let's find out how you—the 3,000 people in the audience this evening—voted on our resolution as you entered the hall. "Be it resolved, American democracy is in its worst crisis in a generation and Donald J. Trump is to blame." Let's see those results. The pre-debate vote: 67 percent agree; 33 percent disagree. This debate is very much in play, perhaps more so than some of our debaters thought going into tonight's contest here in downtown Toronto.

Let's go to our second question, because we always want to see how fluid the debate is, how fluid people's minds are here: Could you potentially switch your vote depending on what you hear over the next hour and a half? Let's see those numbers. Is this audience in play? Eighty percent of you said yes. A very open-minded group here tonight. This is going to be fun! I always love that second vote at the end of the evening, which will let us know which of these teams wins the debate.

Let's begin with opening statements. As is the tradition in debating, we begin with the "pro" side. Andrew Sullivan, your six minutes begin now.

ANDREW SULLIVAN: Ladies and gentlemen, thank you for having me. I come here to tell you something that in your hearts you already know. The United States is in a state of emergency. This emergency began on January 20 of this year. It began because we have a president uniquely unfit to hold office, a president who represents a threat to the core values of American democracy and the stability of the country — a threat to the national security of the United States and to the world. Those are big words, I know. So, let me briefly tell you why I passionately and sincerely believe that statement. The first is that this president has waged a war on the truth from the minute he took office. And throughout the campaign beforehand, for that matter. He lies and he lies and he lies. The *Washington Post* counted 1,300 falsehoods that he has uttered since he became president of the United States, none of which has he retracted. From the idiotic claim that his inauguration crowd was the biggest in history, which you can see by aerial photographs or by your own bare eyes is simply not true, to a lie so dangerous — that three million people voted illegally in the last election — it attacks the very core and the heart and the integrity of our democracy itself.

He is unfit because he has violated and wants to violate and has no respect for the rule of law. This is a president who has told the police to abuse suspects as they arrest them; who has told the military that they should torture suspects — the worse, the better. Even if they're innocent, "They deserve it," he said. He has encouraged violence against people who dare to protest and heckle his crowds, and offered to pay the legal fees of those who commit crimes to assault protestors.

He is still seething with fury every day because his attorney general, Jeff Sessions, one of the most hard-core Republicans you could find, actually dared to recuse himself from an investigation into a campaign with which he was intimately involved. He asked the FBI director to declare his personal loyalty to Trump — not to the rule of law, but to Trump. And when he refused, Trump fired him. And after he fired him, he went on television to brag that that's why he fired the FBI director.

This is a man who has no understanding of, and indeed contempt for the Constitution of the United States; a man who despises the First Amendment; a man who threatened

Jeff Bezos, the owner of the *Washington Post*, with an anti-trust action if his newspaper criticized the president. This is a man who this week said he would remove the licence of NBC because it dared report the truth about what he had said in an insane session about nuclear weapons, after which his own secretary of state called him an f-ing moron.

On national security, this is a man who taunts like a schoolyard kid, a dictator with nuclear weapons, holding the lives of hundreds of thousands of people in his hands, with the responsibility of a teenager chatting on 4chan. This is a man who has undermined NATO, the core of our alliance. This is a man who has declared there is absolute moral equivalence between the United States and Vladimir Putin, the foul dictator. This is a man whom the Republican chairman of the Senate Committee on Foreign Relations has said could drag us into World War III; the same chairman has also described the White House as an adult daycare centre in which adults have to permanently be on shift.

This is fundamentally a man with no sense of responsibility for the power he holds and the sacred duty that he is required to uphold. He will use that power, that office, with everything that has come before it, something that hundreds of thousands of Americans have died for, in order to launch petty, vindictive attacks on private citizens, despoiling the very seat he sits in. He is a man, ladies and gentlemen, who is not in control of himself but who is in control of us.

I wish this were not the case. There are many problems in America that predate him. There are many sins on the left in overreacting to him. There are stupid, multicultural excesses that we can rightly excoriate. There was an elite that refused to understand the stresses that trade and mass immigration have put on the American working classes. All of that is true, and none of it is pertinent to this debate tonight.

This debate is about the worst possible response to those causes and those legitimate feelings. This is about a man who has used those feelings for one thing and one thing only: his own pathetic self-aggrandizement. He is a disgrace to the United States of America. He should be removed by all constitutional measures as soon as possible, by the Twenty-fifth Amendment, by those around him who know the threat that he is.

RUDYARD GRIFFITHS: Thank you, Andrew. A very strong opening statement. Kimberley Strassel, you're next.

KIMBERLEY STRASSEL: Well, thank you all for having me. And at the risk of lowering the tenor of the Munk Debates, I would like to introduce a new word here tonight. I have three children. Before I left, I was telling them about this debate and the resolution, and I asked them, "Help me prepare for this. Tell me why you think Donald Trump has been bad for democracy." And they had a struggle articulating an actual reason why, until finally my six-year-old used her favourite word. She said, "He's bad because he's a pooh-pooh-head."

And while Andrew did a much more eloquent version here on stage, using very fiery words, that sums up what I believe my debate opponents will say tonight. They don't like Donald Trump because he is a "pooh-pooh-head." They will claim that he is divisive. They will argue that he has violated all of the political norms. They will say that he has no respect for his office. They will say that he has undermined America's relationship with the rest of the world. And in all of that, they are largely right.

But that has nothing to do with democracy. Democracy is not just that we don't like someone. Democracy is a very formal concept. It is government for the people and by the people. And in the United States, it's even something more specific. It's documents. The Declaration of Independence. Life, liberty, and the pursuit of happiness. Freedom from a tyrannical government that overtaxes and overregulates. It's the Constitution. And it's the saying that we are a government of laws and not of men; that we have a separation of powers. The Congress makes laws, the executive enforces them, the judiciary interprets them.

Donald Trump was elected because his predecessor violated that Constitution day after day in a lawless fashion. And the backlash that grew in the United States put him in office precisely because he ran as the law-and-order candidate. It was his predecessor, Barack Obama, when frustrated that he couldn't get his people confirmed through the Senate, who declared the Senate out of session. It took the Supreme Court, voting 9–0, to tell him that that was an egregious abuse of the separation of powers.

It was Barack Obama who came to office with a climate program and plans for immigration reform. He acknowledged that he needed Congress to change the laws to make that happen. And when Congress wouldn't do it, he retreated to his office and began to govern by executive fiat.

It was Barack Obama who had a secretary of state who believed that she didn't have to follow the laws of public oversight the way everyone else does, who set up a secret server, and destroyed her emails when people asked to see what she'd done in that office. It was the prior government that seized assets through civil forfeiture laws, taking some five billion dollars; that sicced the IRS on Americans and silenced the voices of tens of thousands of Americans because of their political beliefs.

The current president makes a lot of threats. But as the saying goes, sticks and stones can break your bones but words cannot hurt you. The real measure is whether or not he has actually done anything. And if you look at the policies — and, yes, he is still having some trouble with that legislative agenda. Fair enough. But what Donald Trump threatened with CBS and NBC is nothing compared to Barack Obama, who had his attorney general seize and look through the emails of James Rosen at Fox News — an egregious violation of the First Amendment.

Donald Trump has put people in office that ran against these campaigns, law-and-order candidates who are there to make sure that we restore democracy to what it was before by getting rid of regulations that placed crushing burdens on businesses, and with a new tax code that doesn't reward only those who can afford the best accountants.

This is about fundamental change and restoration of the rule of law. But you don't have to take my word for it.

I was looking in the newspaper just the other day and I found an article in the *Washington Post* with the headline, "How Donald Trump Is Helping Save Our Democracy," written by E. J. Dionne. My first thought was, "Why am I flying to Canada when he's already agreed with me?"

But the point is that, even on the basis of what E. J. and Andrew would argue—that somehow this president is corrosive for our culture—they too think that there could be benefits to Trump. If it is causing more Americans to debate and to pay more attention, then in the end we could end up with an even stronger civil society than we have now.

But, again, this is a president who was brought to office by Americans who wanted to see a return to actual law and order. And anyone who would suggest to you that that's not happening behind the scenes is paying too much attention to a media that's only interested in all the bright and shiny things that Donald Trump says and not what his administration is actually doing. Thank you.

RUDYARD GRIFFITHS: Thank you, Kimberley. E. J. Dionne, your six minutes is on the clock.

E. J. DIONNE: I was standing here while Andrew was speaking and I said a little prayer of thanks for such a vigorous argument on our side of the debate. And I am very grateful to Kim for mentioning that piece I wrote, because I did indeed argue that Donald Trump could be great for our democracy. He could be great for our democracy because he is rallying so many Americans to political action to oppose the very abuses that Andrew opposed. I ask you tonight to take that 67 percent and make it 80 percent, to send a signal to those Americans who know the threat that Donald Trump poses to our democracy that they have friends north of the border.

I want to say it's a great honour to be a guest on this side of the longest undefended border in the world. May it stay that way. May there be no walls between the United States and Canada. We have stood with each other, but perhaps, more importantly, we have learned from each other. Everyone wants a neighbour who embodies decency, and we Americans are very lucky to have you.

And, as you can tell from my last name, my family headed south from Quebec. *Alors, il faut dire merci à vous tous.*

And I do want to salute the courage of our opponents to show up tonight after the week that Donald Trump has had. They clearly have a commitment to the idea that the show must go on.

This is a week in which Donald Trump challenged the very idea of a free press. It bothered him that people can write whatever they want, which sounds like the First Amendment to me. He threatened a network he didn't like with the removal of their licence, which had two problems with it. One is that networks aren't licensed in the first place, and the other is that the threat of using presidential power against people you disagree with is not the mark of a democrat but of an autocrat. And then he told our fellow citizens in Puerto Rico that he might just walk away and allow them to suffer.

So, yes, I salute the bravery of our opponents here. But I want to point out that throughout this debate they will cling to one piece of this resolution like a life raft. They will talk about all the problems the United States has had for five, ten, twenty, or thirty years. And Andrew and I will not for a moment dispute that the United States had problems before Donald Trump and will continue to have some problems after him. Our opponents will try, as Kim just did, to blame everything that's wrong on liberals, on Barack Obama, or on Hillary Clinton. They will do everything in their power to avoid the central issue of this debate, because deep down I think they know that so much of what Donald Trump says and does is indefensible. They will blame everyone else for a crisis that Donald Trump has created.

We are talking about the danger of autocracy. We did not talk about that under George W. Bush or Barack Obama. We are talking about the collapse of the norms of democracy. We did not talk about that before Donald Trump. We are talking, as Andrew outlined, about persistent lying. We did not talk about this before Donald Trump. And, yes, we are talking about what Senator Bob Corker, an early Trump supporter, said of a president in need of an adult daycare centre. This is a crisis for our democracy. We have never had a president who, from his very first day in office, plainly showed that he had no business being president.

Andrew has spoken eloquently about President Trump's threats to our liberty. I want to talk briefly about norms. Norms are the things that you need people to live by, because you cannot write rules for everything.

We could start with the most basic norm, which is truth-telling. Daniel Dale, the great reporter for the *Toronto Star*, just reported today that President Trump, and I quote him, "got a new personal record for the most false claims in a week." That's an amazing record. By Daniel Dale's count, Trump clocked in at forty. And those 1,300 lies or misleading statements that Andrew described amounted to five statements a day. That is quite a record.

Please do not let our opponents in this debate hold democracy to a lower standard. I know they hold democracy to a high standard, and I hope we can persuade even them tonight that it is their job to stand up for our democratic life.

Trump arouses anger, but he also arouses fear — fear about whether our institutions can survive a leader who praises strongmen abroad and sees them as a model for bold leadership. The United States has not faced as grave a threat to its democratic values and its Republican institutions for many decades. Donald Trump is to blame. Thank you.

RUDYARD GRIFFITHS: Thank you, E. J. We are now ready for our last opening statement. Speaker Gingrich, we are going to put six minutes up on the clock. The stage is yours.

NEWT GINGRICH: Well, first of all, I thought that Andrew was spectacular. I thought that the rhythm, the litany, the pattern — it could have been a Shakespearean speech, a condemnation of the tyrant, of a vicious, unending problem. Go back and listen to that sometime, since it is available online, and just listen to the rhythm. His Oxford education gives him such an extraordinary advantage. In

America, if you sound like him you have a twenty-point-higher IQ by virtue of being able to speak.

My good friend E. J. continues the great tradition of the American elite media, which is: they hated Trump before he ran, they hated Trump while he ran, they hated Trump when he was sworn in, and this morning they still hate Trump.

I am going to pose a question for all of you that's a real problem for a free society: How would you know?

A four-star general in the Marine Corps, retired, who lost his son in active duty, went to the press corps in Washington today and said, "So much of what you report is false that it is an enormous problem."

Another four-star general, Chief of Staff John Kelly, retired, serving as secretary of defense, said yesterday that the media reports about Trump wanting to have a tenfold increase in nuclear weapons are totally false.

Now, you may decide they have both been infected, as my friends would suggest. They have become Trump-ized; they no longer know the truth. Or you may decide that a great deal of what you believe is total hogwash, brought to you by a news media which is so deep into its own incestuous ideology and its own way of keeping score that it hasn't a clue what Donald Trump is doing, because it cannot allow itself to think openly and objectively. I'll give you some examples.

Trump's speech in Warsaw is an extraordinary document. It's comparable to Reagan. And I say that with some knowledge because Tony Dolan, who was Reagan's chief speechwriter, helped write it and said this was equal to anything Reagan ever said in defence of Western civilization. But, of course, if you are on the left, the very idea that you would defend Western civilization is probably proof that there is something wrong.

Read Trump's United Nations speech, which has a core argument—you may disagree with the argument, but it's not trivial. He says the base of freedom starts with sovereignty. If the United Nations is a collection of sovereign countries who then reach agreements, it's useful. If, however, we're moving toward a globalization with a bureaucratic, legalistic system in which our nations are merely subordinate parts of this larger thing, then it's stunningly dangerous.

I headed, along with George Mitchell, the former Democratic leader of the Senate, a three-year study of the United Nations. Now, I don't know about you, but to me the idea that the General Assembly should replace the Canadian Parliament or the American Congress as a source of ultimate authority is insane. Look at who belongs to it. Look at who is on the Human Rights Commission. If you're not a tyrant or a dictator, you're not allowed on.

So, they all get together to say, "Hey, we're doing fine but, of course, Israel should be condemned." Israel is condemned a hundred times a year—"Oh, it must be Tuesday. Can we go condemn Israel?" Now, you wouldn't want to condemn Venezuela or Cuba or Zimbabwe. You certainly wouldn't want to consider what the Chinese are doing to create a truly totalitarian system of information in which they are now tracking every cellphone in China. "Oh, that would be inappropriate." So, I think what Trump was saying was very profound.

Look at what Trump is doing to deregulate. You can agree or disagree, but he is returning power to the states. He is returning power to local communities. He is actually following the law. And I know from my friends over here who claim they worry about democracy that the great number of executive orders that were illegal and unconstitutional were signed by Barack Obama. They were not signed by Donald Trump.

So, there are profound differences. But there is a simple problem underway. The American people rebelled. This is not a local thing. It's happening in Austria. It happened in the city of Rome, which elected its first woman mayor in 2,500 years of history. It's happening in Catalonia. You can't blame all of these things on Trump. Angela Merkel just had the worst election since 1946 for the conservative parties in Germany. People are unhappy around the planet. Well, they were unhappy in the U.S. and they decided that the source of their unhappiness was Washington and they wanted somebody who would kick over the table. So, here we are. Trump's draining the swamp. The alligators are unhappy — and two of the lead alligators are here tonight on the defence.

RUDYARD GRIFFITHS: Let's hear from those two hungry alligators. We are now going into our rebuttals. We're putting three minutes on the clock and we're going to hear from the "pro" side first. Andrew, let's go to you first for your rebuttal of your opponents' opening statements.

ANDREW SULLIVAN: Yes, I am very, very glad to. I am going to take specific points that were made and attempt to address them. The first is that everything that I cited is some invention of the liberal media. The truth is that almost everything I cited is in the public record — on television. Trump's quotes are there to track, to look at, and to examine. There is nothing here that is thin, and everything that I cited was fact.

Now, one of the things that autocrats do is mix lies with facts endlessly. They "gaslight" people. They pretend — and autocrats always do this — that a free press is the real danger to society. I side with Thomas Jefferson, and not with Vladimir Putin and Donald Trump. A free press is essential. And in America, we have a conservative press and a conservative media, as well as a liberal press and a liberal media. The facts this time are on the liberal media's side.

I will concede that Barack Obama did commit and execute executive orders that were out of line. He did so because from day one he was faced with the Republican Party's insane decision to do nothing but obstruct everything he attempted. Even when he was inheriting the worst recession since the 1930s, they didn't give him a single vote for a surplus.

Now, with a much greater debt, they are proposing another con to borrow more money to pay for tax cuts, not for the middle class, but for the wealthy. And they claim once again that it will decrease the deficit rather than increase it.

I will note that, yes, when you look on paper some people can write speeches. Some people are smart in the White

House, even though Stephen Miller isn't exactly Arthur Schlesinger. They can write some eloquent speeches. I also listened to the speech, the inaugural speech—a cavalcade of hatred and fear and demonization. A man who, by democratic standards, Kimberley, actually lost the popular vote.

He is rightly president because our constitutional republic has rules that require him to be president. And I accept completely his legitimacy, and have done so from day one. But it's precisely those rules of a constitutional republic that he threatens.

Thirdly, I want to point out that Speaker Gingrich is correct, and I agree with him, that globalization has gone too far and too fast.

RUDYARD GRIFFITHS: E. J., you're up next—alligator number two.

E. J. DIONNE: If Andrew and I are defenders of the swamp, then Mr. Gingrich is here on behalf of the Socialist International! Trump has taken the swamp and added in many new alligators and polluted the swamp far more than it ever has been polluted before. It is Mr. Trump's cabinet secretaries who have flown around on charter planes at the taxpayer's expense when they could have just as easily taken a car or a train from Washington to Philadelphia and gotten there much more quickly.

It is Donald Trump who, uniquely among recent presidents, has refused to release his tax returns so we can know how many millions or billions this tax cut proposal he is pushing might save him. It is Donald Trump who has refused to separate himself from his businesses, unlike any president in recent memory. And while we don't know what is happening in his businesses, we do know that somehow there are more members of his golf clubs than ever and all kinds of influential people wanting to stay in his hotels.

The ways in which the swamp is far more polluted than when Mr. Trump got there are legion. As Andrew pointed out, it is not the media who has made up the things we are saying about Donald Trump. Almost everything we are saying that is wrong with Donald Trump has come out of Donald Trump's own mouth.

It is Donald Trump who said that rather authoritarian-sounding thing: "I alone can fix it." It is Donald Trump who said of our American intelligence agencies that they were taking a shot at him and asked, "Are we living in Nazi Germany?" It was Donald Trump who said, "Don't worry about any of my businesses because the president can't have a conflict of interest."

It was Donald Trump who, when the courts ruled against him on his travel ban, tried to blame them for future terrorism. "If something happens, blame him," he said of one of the judges and the court system. It was Donald Trump who falsely said that President Obama had tapped his phones—he spelled it, by the way, T-A-P-P—before the election. It was Donald Trump who said he'd fired the FBI director because of the "Russia thing."

Our case is not based on propaganda. Our case is not based on falsehood. Our case is based on what Donald Trump has said and who he is.

KIMBERLEY STRASSEL: I would like to rebut what E. J. just said: "Our case is based on what Donald Trump has said." If you listen to everything that E. J. and Andrew have mentioned, they cannot name a concrete example of an action that the president has taken to undermine democracy.

Andrew writes on his blog with even more adjectives than he used up here tonight. No one has ever said he cannot do so. But this president has not interfered, and the press is right to engage and obviously to cover him and to say whatever they want, no matter how false it is. It makes me laugh. The press runs constant articles saying that Donald Trump's approval rating is 35 percent. Isn't that horrible? Doesn't that say terrible things about our country? Do you want to know what the United States media's approval rating is? Twelve. So, they really are not in a position to lecture. And that number was there well before Donald Trump came to office.

I defy my opponents to give an example of how Donald Trump has, in the way that Barack Obama did, trampled over the rights of the congressional branch, stripped their powers from it. Name for me one time that the Supreme Court has ruled 9–0 to stop one of his actions.

E. J. just mentioned the lower courts and Trump's travel ban. What he did not mention is that the Supreme Court ultimately upheld the main provisions of it because it was constitutional, because it was legal, in contrast to his predecessor's decision to grant far-flung immunity to illegal immigrants in the United States.

By the way, this is a problem we all have to try to overcome. We have to try to get beyond justifying illegal behaviour just because we agree with the policy. Andrew just said, "Well, why did Barack Obama continually act in a lawless way? Because he was obstructed." Really? Is that your justification? I am sure everyone in this audience would be more than a little alarmed if I said that Chuck Schumer's obstruction in the Senate now gives Donald Trump licence to do whatever he wants and justifies him in that action. That's why we don't like precedents like that.

I'll give you a personal example. At the *Wall Street Journal* editorial page, I have passionately fought for years and years for the rights of Dreamers living in the United States — brought here by no fault of their own, but by their parents — to continue living in the United States and offering all the amazing contributions that they do. Nonetheless, I opposed the way that Barack Obama did it because you don't simply exempt people from the law. We are a nation of laws. Donald Trump is returning us to that. And in the end, as a result, our democracy, our institutions, our rule of law will be stronger, and that's what we need to measure him on.

NEWT GINGRICH: I did think, by the way, E. J., that it was a tactical mistake to bring up the lower court decision by a nutcake judge who was overruled, I think, 8–0 by the Supreme Court, because that's one of the complaints of conservatives about the judicial system. If you look at the Ninth Circuit Court, which is crazy; if you look at some of the individual judges that are out there who are crazy, they do make decisions that are crazy. And, by the way, on national security grounds — and they were just repudiated 8–0 on national security grounds — in the Constitution the president is the commander-in-chief; he has the obligation to take steps to defend America. You can agree or disagree with him, but no judge should interpose themselves in a way that makes America more vulnerable to attack, and then be shocked if the president of the United States says, "You just made America more vulnerable to attack."

Now, you said that this was somehow inappropriate; it's not at all inappropriate. Franklin Delano Roosevelt attacked the courts. Thomas Jefferson attacked the courts. The Jeffersonians' major campaign plank, one of them, was anti-court. And I appreciate Jefferson's appreciation of the media. You know, I have always thought the Jefferson subsidy of a newspaper to attack Hamilton while Hamilton was subsidizing a newspaper to attack Jefferson when they were both serving in the same cabinet was an example of freedom of the press to take bribes from politicians that is worthy of being brought up by people like you. So, I appreciate your bringing up Jefferson.

I also want to remind all of you who worry about dissent in America that one of the most popular musicals of modern times is based on the vice president of the United States shooting the secretary of the treasury. We have not had, since Hamilton, a single incident of such passion, and therefore I feel comfortable that America will endure and succeed in absorbing all of this.

But let me go a step further. Two quick things, if I have time. The first was something Andrew said that I think you should think about in terms of its viciousness and its dishonesty; that is the clever mixing together of Putin and Trump. Let's be clear: Vladimir Putin was trained by the KGB. He believes in torturing and killing people. His government routinely assassinates people. He kills reporters who write the wrong things. He has imposed in many ways a vicious dictatorship. He is involved in attacking eastern Ukraine. He has seized Crimea. And to suggest that there is anything in the American system comparable to Putin is profoundly dishonest intellectually and makes it impossible to have a rational, reasonable discussion. Because now if you accept the two words in the same phrase, you're already in a crazy environment. So, I think that's bad.

Lastly, one quick example of the real hostility to freedom in America. At William & Mary College two weeks ago, Black Lives Matter protestors surrounded an ACLU spokesperson, would not let her speak physically, and walled her off from her audience on the grounds that she had no right to be there. The most violence in America today is on the left, not the right.

RUDYARD GRIFFITHS: Thank you, debaters, for a terrific opening to this debate. You've set the table; let's now dig into some of the specific issues. I think we all agree this debate has a political dimension to it, an economic dimension, and a cultural dimension. And let me start with you, Andrew, and pick up on Kimberley's point, because I think it was an important one in her rebuttal. We disagree with many things that Trump says—many of us in this audience, viscerally, by the noises that the crowd has made.

But give us a specific, concrete action that has resulted from this president that has undermined the institutions, the values, the norms of American democracy.

ANDREW SULLIVAN: I'll give you a simple example that is a direct equivalent to the Obama situation. And I'm not defending Obama. I think he did abuse the executive privilege.

KIMBERLEY STRASSEL: But you justified him.

ANDREW SULLIVAN: I didn't.

KIMBERLEY STRASSEL: You said it was okay because he was obstructed.

ANDREW SULLIVAN: No. I said that was the context in which it happened. I still don't think it was defensible. But I don't think Obama's intent and the way he behaved as president is anything like as dangerous to democracy and democratic values as Donald Trump.

Here is a classic example. This is the man who has faced obstructionism in Congress from his own party, who has been unable to construct a workable majority for any of the proposals that he has constructed. The fact that he is too incompetent to be a dictator doesn't mean his will and his intent are not there.

KIMBERLEY STRASSEL: So, the example?

ANDREW SULLIVAN: The fact that the constitutional order of the United States, which has lasted 240 years, has not collapsed after nine months is not a great achievement, despite his great efforts.

KIMBERLEY STRASSEL: No, we guard it.

ANDREW SULLIVAN: But here is how he acted. And let me take the key law that he has been trying to pass now for nine months and been incapable of doing so, and that is the health care law, the Affordable Care Act, which is the law of the land. And he is required to effectively enforce the law of the land. He has been unable to change the law of the land, so what is he doing? He is sabotaging it. He is using his office to sabotage and undermine the laws of the land at the expense of potentially millions of people's health insurance and health care. Now, that seems to me sabotaging things when he can't change them. The same thing with the Iran deal.

RUDYARD GRIFFITHS: Okay, hold on. We're going to stop there. Before we get to Iran, we'll have Kimberley respond to this. Does that meet your litmus test?

KIMBERLEY STRASSEL: It's awfully hard to sabotage a law that's collapsing under its own weight.

ANDREW SULLIVAN: There is no evidence of that whatsoever.

KIMBERLEY STRASSEL: When you have entire counties across the United States that no longer have any more than one option for their health care. When people are watching their premiums triple or quadruple. When average basic business owners can no longer afford to get health care.

ANDREW SULLIVAN: I would have no health care at all without Obamacare, thank you.

KIMBERLEY STRASSEL: Well, many people have no health care *because* of it. So, we can all agree that it's not—

ANDREW SULLIVAN: That is absolutely false.

E. J. DIONNE: That is a falsehood. Many Americans *have* health care because of Obamacare.

KIMBERLEY STRASSEL: I can name members of my family who don't have health care because of it. They had it perfectly fine before Obamacare came in, but now they no longer have it. The bigger point, though, is that it's hard to sabotage it—

ANDREW SULLIVAN: It's hard to sabotage it?

KIMBERLEY STRASSEL: It's hard to sabotage something that's already failing, okay?

ANDREW SULLIVAN: But Trump is trying, right?

RUDYARD GRIFFITHS: Hold on. Let Kimberley finish her point.

KIMBERLEY STRASSEL: It's hard to sabotage something that's failing. But also, you're talking of the law of the land; this is a law that the former president unilaterally changed more than forty-two times himself. This has now become such an elastic definition of what the law is that nobody knows what it is anymore because the prior president didn't respect his own law.

ANDREW SULLIVAN: A law sets up an institution and a mechanism with regulations. And the regulations to enforce that law are a part of the interest of the executive branch, to make sure that that law is properly enforced.

KIMBERLEY STRASSEL: And to the extent that he kept changing the regulations, it was an abuse of his executive power.

ANDREW SULLIVAN: The last president attempted to use his executive power to enforce that law. The current president is using his executive power to undermine that law.

KIMBERLEY STRASSEL: Right. Why is it not an abuse for Obama to use that power when it is an abuse for Donald Trump?

RUDYARD GRIFFITHS: Hold on a sec. This is a debate about American democracy, not a debate about American health care.

KIMBERLEY STRASSEL: That's not a concrete example.

E. J. DIONNE: No, but it's about undermining the law.

I want to pick up on something Newt said, that this notion that Andrew invented the link between Vladimir Putin and Donald Trump was somehow intellectually dishonest. It was not Andrew Sullivan; it was Donald Trump who said that Vladimir Putin, the man you said was a KGB agent, was a stronger leader than Barack Obama. It was not Andrew Sullivan who said that.

NEWT GINGRICH: Well, that's technically true.

E. J. DIONNE: It was Donald Trump who refused over and over again to say a critical word about Vladimir Putin in his campaign. You want actions Trump took? Trump fired James Comey because he got too close to the "Russia thing." That is an action that is genuinely troubling in this administration: Donald Trump upbraiding his attorney general because the attorney general refused to recuse himself from a case that he was plainly involved in.

KIMBERLEY STRASSEL: But the recusal happened.

E. J. DIONNE: These are intimations of autocratic behaviour.

RUDYARD GRIFFITHS: Let's pause for a second, because that is an interesting example E. J. is highlighting of a specific action that he's alleging the president has undertaken that has directly harmed American democracy. Newt, respond to it.

NEWT GINGRICH: I'm not sure which part of that you mean. He said, in a setting where a large number of conservatives may agree, the term is "stronger leader." That's one thing.

ANDREW SULLIVAN: No, no. Let me follow up with that. He said on television, when he was actually presented with a point you just made, that Vladimir Putin is a killer.

KIMBERLEY STRASSEL: How does this undermine democracy?

ANDREW SULLIVAN: And he responded, Kimberley — and I know you don't want to hear this — but he responded, "Well, we are killers, too. We kill people as well."

KIMBERLEY STRASSEL: How does this undermine —

ANDREW SULLIVAN: Now, if any Democrat had said such a thing, you would impeach the guy.

NEWT GINGRICH: We'd be unhappy.

E. J. DIONNE: Jeane Kirkpatrick talked about moral equivalence. I have never heard a worse case of moral equivalence in the state.

ANDREW SULLIVAN: But can you, Speaker Gingrich, launch an impeachment of a president because he committed perjury in a civil trial? But a president who admits obstruction of justice in public is someone you want to praise?

NEWT GINGRICH: He didn't obstruct justice.

ANDREW SULLIVAN: Where is your consistency?

NEWT GINGRICH: Wait a second. This is something which Andy McCarthy, as a former prosecutor for the federal government, has outlined clearly. Presidents have the authority to fire the FBI director, period. It's in the Constitution. He's the chief executive, period.

ANDREW SULLIVAN: Yes, they do. But not as obstruction of justice. Not to quash an investigation into his own campaign.

NEWT GINGRICH: What's quashed? Mueller is out there with seventeen lawyers running around with a grand jury—

ANDREW SULLIVAN: Despite Trump, not because of him.

NEWT GINGRICH: But he's out there.

ANDREW SULLIVAN: Yes, because in fact—

KIMBERLEY STRASSEL: Democracy is working.

NEWT GINGRICH: So, your argument is that Trump is such a powerful autocrat, but he's so incompetent that he can't be autocratically autocratic because he's too incompetent. So, all the things you are worried about aren't happening because he is not smart enough to stop them. Because the fact is, the investigation *is* underway. It's underway in the Senate. It's underway in the House. It's underway in the Justice Department. It's underway at the *Washington Post*. It's underway at the *New York Times*. It's underway at NBC News. But we're supposedly in danger of America losing its freedom because of an incompetent person who can't achieve any of the things that you're worried about? I just want to understand.

ANDREW SULLIVAN: When a president openly hopes for an investigation and fires someone to obstruct an investigation under the rule of law; when he seethes with anger at an attorney general because he obeys the rule of law; when he tells police officers to break the law; when he tells U.S. service members to break the law, his words matter, Speaker Gingrich. His words are acts. And his words continually undermine the rule of law and the Constitution of the United States.

KIMBERLEY STRASSEL: This is where we've now come: "His words are acts" because — listen closely — Andrew could not come up with anything that he has done other than that he used his executive power.

E. J. DIONNE: Wait.

KIMBERLEY STRASSEL: No. He used his executive power in health care in the exact same way that Barack Obama did. Somehow that's supposedly wrong?

ANDREW SULLIVAN: No. He has not faithfully executed—

KIMBERLEY STRASSEL: So, now we've moved to "words are acts." Okay, that's simply not true. And also, the entire way the media has completely changed around this Russia probe story is incredible to me. James Comey was aware that the president was not himself under investigation. The president asked several times for James Comey to clarify that. He refused to do it because James Comey was a political player in Washington.

ANDREW SULLIVAN: No, because James Comey—

KIMBERLEY STRASSEL: And now we know that he was keeping secret memos, that he leaked things to the press. Look, if you want to talk about things that should scare people about democracy, how about the head of the FBI actively investigating both candidates for the presidency simultaneously with the use of a secret court and wireless warrant. That is concerning.

And now that we are attempting to exercise some oversight and find out exactly what happened there and what inspired such a probe and what actions were taken, all kinds of obstruction is happening, but not from the Trump administration. From the career bureaucrats left over from the past administration.

E. J. DIONNE: I want to say a couple of things.

RUDYARD GRIFFITHS: We'll take E. J.'s comments.

E. J. DIONNE: First, I think Andrew and I have already made progress because Newt conceded that Trump has not been an effective authoritarian because of his incompetence. So, we have the incompetence of Donald Trump on the table already. But I think what Kim said is incredibly dangerous. What she just did, what Trump supporters do all the time — and it is why we are concerned about the role of truth in our politics — is that she has ascribed all sorts of evil motives to James Comey, who, if we know anything about what he did, intervened in the election in a way that hurt Hillary Clinton. And he did not come out with any information about the Donald Trump investigation that was ongoing. Comey was not willing to make a statement before the investigation was over.

We know from the Mueller investigation that they have not closed off the idea that Donald Trump was involved in this. They have not settled the matter. The attack on James Comey is of a piece with what Andrew and I are worried about. And Donald Trump was vocally upset when Sessions recused himself. And there would not be a special counsel if the deputy attorney general had not insisted.

And what we are concerned about, and the reason we worry about our democracy, is that we don't know what is going to happen at the end. We do not know if there will be a Saturday Night Massacre; if the equivalent of Elliot Richardson will be fired in this case. Donald Trump's behaviour up until now can give one no confidence that we will avoid that path this time.

RUDYARD GRIFFITHS: Speaker Gingrich?

NEWT GINGRICH: Let's go back and look at Comey for a minute. When Comey was the number two person under Bush, he appointed a special counsel for what he knew was not a crime; for what involved leaking a name from the CIA, which they knew at the time was not a crime. And they knew who leaked it. And they told the person who leaked it to shut up. And they appointed a special counsel who tried to get Vice President Cheney, and couldn't get him, and in the end, managed to get somebody who was a totally decent civil servant on a technical argument.

Now, this is where Mueller is going to end up going. Mueller will get somebody. You don't get seventeen high-priced lawyers, virtually all of whom voted for Hillary, virtually all of whom donated to Hillary — you don't get those kinds of lawyers in a room to change their career, come to work as part of a task force, and not get somebody.

E. J. DIONNE: So, you are already trying to discredit an ongoing investigation and setting us up so that when Trump fires him you'll say this was political. That's what I'm worried about.

NEWT GINGRICH: Can I finish?

ANDREW SULLIVAN: This attack on the possibility of neutral enforcement of the laws by career professionals, by someone whose reputation has stood up to Republican presidents, including George W. Bush, at great risk to his own career—

NEWT GINGRICH: Wait! Let me just finish.

KIMBERLEY STRASSEL: You know when I last heard that argument? I last heard it when Comey was investigating Hillary Clinton—

RUDYARD GRIFFITHS: Woah, woah, woah. If you're all talking at once, the audience cannot hear any one of you individually. The Speaker has the floor.

NEWT GINGRICH: I was just going to bring it to the present. It is Comey who, under oath in the Senate, said, "Oh yes, I deliberately leaked a memo through a friend of mine who is a professor at Columbia," knowing the *New York Times* would publish it and it would force the appointment of a special counsel. Now when the—

E. J. DIONNE: Because he was afraid that Trump was going to obstruct—

NEWT GINGRICH: I don't care why. Wait a second, E. J. I don't care what the cause is. The guy who was the director of the FBI telling you he broke the law, which he did, by leaking—

E. J. DIONNE: He did not break the law. There was no law broken.

NEWT GINGRICH: Oh, so it's all right to leak memos for the purpose of —

E. J. DIONNE: You see, there was no law broken by what Comey did.

ANDREW SULLIVAN: Notice, ladies and gentleman, how the argument has been diverted — how we are now engaged in a character assassination of one of the most honourable people who has ever served in Washington. Because an autocrat, a man who cannot tolerate any opposition, a man who resists any non-zero-sum engagement, a man who cannot tolerate the slightest criticism without acting on revenge has infected the minds, the souls, of these people so they are attacking the integrity of the very process of democracy. That's how deep the rot has gone.

RUDYARD GRIFFITHS: I'm going to let Kimberley respond to that rather pointed attack.

KIMBERLEY STRASSEL: I do remember that the last time I heard a group of people who were just incensed over the abuses of a career bureaucrat and the licence he was taking with his office was the entire left-wing establishment and press when James Comey decided to come out and criticize Hillary Clinton in public in the middle of an election.

ANDREW SULLIVAN: Not me, Kimberley. Not me. Prove it.

KIMBERLEY STRASSEL: Then you were alone in that, because everyone else was out there—

ANDREW SULLIVAN: Well, I'm here to defend myself, not to be truncated by guilt by association.

KIMBERLEY STRASSEL: So, please don't suggest that it's just conservatives or those here on the stage that are now questioning the integrity of James Comey. We all know that people in powerful positions also need to be held to account. It is very concerning that you have an FBI director who is now so vigorously opposing any oversight of what he did. And we have lost our way—

RUDYARD GRIFFITHS: Okay, I think we have relitigated the Comey affair. We've got a lot of topics to cover and we've spent significant time on this. Let's all sit down for a moment, okay? Take a collective breath and move on to the next aspect of this debate.

I want to pick up on something that Speaker Gingrich said in his rebuttal, which is an argument that you are going to no doubt have a strong response to. And that is that the crisis of democracy in America today, according to Speaker Gingrich's camp, is a crisis of the Left, a view that identity politics in the Left—safe spaces, microaggressions, a whole litany of ideas about how America should be reconfigured and restructured—that these are what has precipitated this acute moment in American culture; that this crisis resides with the Left, not with the Right.

E. J. DIONNE: I have known Speaker Gingrich for about thirty years, and in times of high unemployment or low unemployment, in times of national concord and national discord, he has always said that the problems in American politics come from the Left.

NEWT GINGRICH: Yes.

E. J. DIONNE: So, I don't think that that should surprise us in the least.

I just want to make a point about this extended discussion we had just now. It proved the central point that Andrew and I were trying to make, which is that our opponents in this debate have to keep diverting you from what Trump has actually done.

They do not want any of us talking about the fact that it is Republicans like Bob Corker who are very worried about the possibility of World War III. And it is Republicans and Congress who privately say that they are worried about many of the same aspects of Donald Trump's personality, his approach to issues, his tempestuousness, his lack of focus. Instead, we talked about a man named James Comey. It's Donald Trump who is on trial here today in this proposition.

Secondly, if we want to have a long debate over problems in the American economy, about the problems of inequality, we could have a very long debate about that, and I would

73

welcome it. But I do not think it is the left side of American politics that is dividing us in the way Donald Trump did on the day of Charlottesville, when he tried to create a moral equivalence between Klansmen and Nazis and those who opposed him. Because many of those who were standing there in the streets opposing them were peaceful protestors trying to oppose the lies of this Far Right.

And look at the lies of the Far Right itself. I believe that this movement has empowered new forms of political action on the right, the Far Right end of politics, that I know Kim and Newt have to oppose in their hearts and in their consciences. And I think this should worry us. And when we see these movements empowered in our country and given airing, it is not just bad for liberals, it is bad for the entire conservative movement as well.

NEWT GINGRICH: Let me be clear about what E. J. was just saying. No one on the left wants to take the student violence in Connecticut, where they actually injured a professor to stop a conservative from speaking. Nobody on the left wants to take the people, the Antifa people at Berkeley, who have said they are eager to use violence to stop people from speaking.

Nobody on the left wants to confront the fact that in the latest study, professors under thirty-five are by a ratio of 12:1 Democrats, and the idea of your getting tenure if you're a conservative is a joke.

No one on the left wants to look at the kind of language I described a minute ago, where Black Lives Matter pro- testors — and I thought it was ironic — literally blocked an ACLU spokesperson from speaking at William & Mary, physically blocked her, and then blocked her from seeing the audience, so she couldn't even mingle with the people who came out to talk to her.

Now, nobody on the left wants to deal with this. Nobody on the left wants to deal with the degree to which Soros is funding network after network, which is designed to undermine democracy and create exactly the kind of violence I just described.

E. J. DIONNE: Ah, the spectre of George Soros! We can't talk about Trump; we have got to talk about George Soros now —

NEWT GINGRICH: I rest my case. You cannot talk factually about what's going on in America and have them take it seriously, because it totally discredits their case.

RUDYARD GRIFFITHS: Andrew?

ANDREW SULLIVAN: You may know, Speaker Gingrich, and you may know, Kimberley, that I have been very vocal and consistently vocal against this poison on the left. I do it every week. I do it in venues where I am likely to get a lot of blowback. I do it at great risk to my career and my job. You're right: there is an awful poison on the left. There is a poison that is dividing this country. And it's a poison that's increasing racial divides, not ameliorating them. And there are also — E. J. is right, obviously — some foul, disgusting, far-right movements in this country.

My point is simply this, and it's about Donald Trump: He is president of the United States. It is his job, his responsibility, to attempt to bridge the divide, not to exploit it, deepen it, and make it much worse.

KIMBERLEY STRASSEL: I think that if you are familiar with my work, then you also know that I have spent years writing about the scary abuse of government power and the attempt of people to silence their political opponents using not just tactics such as Speaker Gingrich was talking about, but far more scary ones. So, I know something about abuse of government power and words like "autocrats" and "tyranny."

Let me give you an example of something that happened in the United States just a few years ago. In Wisconsin, a liberal district attorney was mad at conservative groups that had supported a Republican governor. He launched a bogus campaign finance investigation into these thirty groups under a law in Wisconsin called the John Doe law. It allowed him to do it in secret and to impose a gag order on everyone who was being investigated. They had their financial records taken, their emails taken. There were pre-dawn raids staged on their homes. In one case involving a child of one of the targets — the parents were off on a charitable fundraising trip — the police came, broke into the house, put him in a room, wouldn't allow him to call his lawyer, wouldn't allow him to call his grandparents, and as they left, said, "If you tell anyone what happened to you here this morning, you'll go to jail."

Now, that's an abuse of government power. That happened on the left. And if I saw Donald Trump engaging in anything like that, you can believe me that I would be the first person to say something about it.

But this is ridiculous. To this point we have lots of words: autocracy, tyranny, et cetera. We do not have an example. Even the Jim Comey example. You're not making the case that it was illegal for him to do it.

ANDREW SULLIVAN: It is illegal to obstruct justice, Kimberley.

KIMBERLEY STRASSEL: And nobody has found him to have obstructed justice.

ANDREW SULLIVAN: There is currently an investigation to find out.

KIMBERLEY STRASSEL: But no one has yet come up with anything to suggest that he has actually undermined any democratic institutions or laws.

ANDREW SULLIVAN: I just did.

KIMBERLEY STRASSEL: It's not proven.

E. J. DIONNE: Our opponents want to swim in a sea of red herrings. I have no idea what an investigation in Wisconsin many, many years ago has to do with what's on the table tonight.

KIMBERLEY STRASSEL: No, it was a few years ago. It's government abuse.

E. J. DIONNE: But the pardon of Joe Arpaio, which happened this year and was done by Donald Trump, has a great deal to do with what we're talking about tonight.

KIMBERLEY STRASSEL: I think that's my point, E. J. You didn't care when it was happening in Wisconsin, but now suddenly you have a very fine air about—

ANDREW SULLIVAN: But do *you* care now?

KIMBERLEY STRASSEL: About what happens with democracy?

ANDREW SULLIVAN: Do you care now, Kimberley, about the pardoning of Joe Arpaio? Have you written about it? Don't you consider that a clear violation and abuse of Trump's power?

KIMBERLEY STRASSEL: Pardon power?

ANDREW SULLIVAN: Yes, the pardon power.

E. J. DIONNE: Let's look at Joe Arpaio.

KIMBERLEY STRASSEL: Why is that a violation of the pardon power?

ANDREW SULLIVAN: Do you think it's okay to pardon a public official —

KIMBERLEY STRASSEL: What about Mark Rich?

E. J. DIONNE: Kimberley, I let you have your little excursion to Wisconsin. Let me say something.

Joe Arpaio was accused of violating the constitutional rights of people in Arizona. And Donald Trump tried, at first, to end the investigation, but he couldn't succeed in doing that. So he pardoned a man accused of constitutional violations of the rights of minorities.

Now, this is an action. I am not making this up. This is not what Mr. Gingrich likes to call "the terrible news media." This is a fact. And when a president of the United States uses this rather unlimited pardon power to pardon someone who violates the constitutional rights of American citizens, I don't know whose constitutional rights are safe. Because you remember Martin Niemöller's line, "First they came for these brothers and sisters of ours," and we do not know where that story ends, but it rarely ends well.

NEWT GINGRICH: Let me start with that. This, of course, is referring to the Nazis. My underlying point is, Why did we quote somebody who is talking about the Nazis as a reference to Trump? Now, let me tell you why these guys in the end have —

E. J. DIONNE: I didn't use the word "Nazi." That idea holds whether you were talking about Nazis or whether you were talking about any regime you might worry about.

NEWT GINGRICH: But it's about tyranny.

E. J. DIONNE: I agree. I do not make Nazi metaphors because they are a mistake.

NEWT GINGRICH: All right. But it's about tyranny.

KIMBERLEY STRASSEL: Like Wisconsin.

E. J. DIONNE: Unless they are real Nazis on the streets in Charlottesville.

NEWT GINGRICH: But let me suggest to all of you that in a sense, citing the Arpaio pardon is a perfect example of what we're talking about. You can make a pretty good case that it was a dumb pardon, a bad pardon — that he shouldn't have done it.

E. J. DIONNE: Yeah.

NEWT GINGRICH: That's a policy question.

E. J, DIONNE: Thank you for that.

KIMBERLEY STRASSEL: That's policy.

NEWT GINGRICH: But you had an eighty-five-year-old man who had spent his entire lifetime in law enforcement, who had been re-elected over and over by massive majorities.

I'm assuming those are mostly liberals who are groaning. I understand the absence of compassion for people you don't agree with.

But just think about it from this standpoint. I am not arguing for it; I'm trying to make a deeper point. So, Trump decides that an eighty-five-year-old former lawman probably shouldn't go to jail. Now, some of you would say, "No, by God, what a great chance to show the police nobody is above the law. Let's punish this eighty-five-year-old who is clearly such a danger." That's not the argument we're having tonight. That's a policy argument. You can say that's a really stupid thing to do, but, as a matter of the United States Constitution, there is zero question that the president of the United States can pardon anyone at any time. Zero question.

E. J. DIONNE: And that's why I am so afraid that he will abuse this power — that what he did in Arpaio's case he could do in other cases.

NEWT GINGRICH: But, wait. He may abuse the power, but he won't have broken the law. He won't be an autocrat. He will be doing precisely what the founding fathers wrote into the Constitution to enable the president to do, what they thought he should do. This was not a bunch of stupid people.

ANDREW SULLIVAN: Did the founding fathers believe that if the president—if this turns out to be the case; it's a possibility—finds that people in his campaign broke the law by colluding with Russia in trying to distort the results of the election, and the president decides to pardon them, do you think pardoning his own people, and indeed pardoning himself, is something the founders really thought this power was supposed to be used for?

NEWT GINGRICH: You're making my case. What the founders would have said is that that's why you have the impeachment provision.

KIMBERLEY STRASSEL: Correct.

NEWT GINGRICH: And if it turns out that a president were to pardon himself and the Congress were to decide that was unacceptable, they have the full power to impeach him.

But you're making my case. Everything you just complained about is totally constitutional, was written into the document. He did not in any way abuse his power. He may have done something that was not right in terms of policy, but he did nothing that was wrong in terms of constitutional authority.

ANDREW SULLIVAN: He is actively undermining the spirit of the Constitution, the norms and procedures that are essential to maintaining the Constitution; and he actively, every day, excoriates and exhibits contempt for the notion of a republic under law, in which he is equal, not above everybody else. He fundamentally mistakes the understanding of the presidency in the United States. And he mistakes it in ways that make one extremely nervous, Newt.

You must concede surely, let me beg you, that the rhetoric that this man has used, that his love of Putin, of Duterte—his praise of a man who has extrajudicially killed thousands of people—surely you are troubled by the rhetoric and tone of this person. Surely you are troubled by a president who tells law enforcement officers to abuse suspects. Surely there are some lines you don't want a president to cross.

KIMBERLEY STRASSEL: Of course. There are some things I wish he wouldn't say every single day.

ANDREW SULLIVAN: Well, then why don't you say that—

KIMBERLEY STRASSEL: We do. If you read the editorial page, we do, on nearly a daily basis, point out some of the things he does which we think make him a real "pooh-pooh-head."

But you're making it sound as though the random things that go through Trump's brain become law or action. They do not. Have you met Ryan Zinke, the head of his Interior Department? Have you met Scott Pruitt, the head of his Environmental Protection Agency (EPA)? Have you met any of the people that he's installed in these positions? Because they are the folks who are actually making the decisions and running the government. And many of them are constitutional law professors.

Again, Scott Pruitt, before he was made head of the EPA, led the charge among dozens of states to sue the Obama administration over its own overreach of its powers. These are people with a deeply held belief in federalism and the rule of law. *They* are running the government. And no matter what random things happen in Donald Trump's head, until you can prove to me that they have been put into action, then they are nothing more than your fears and rhetoric.

RUDYARD GRIFFITHS: This has been a terrific debate. I have been virtually superfluous as a moderator and that's always a great sign of a terrific conversation and important issues being tackled.

I'm conscious that we've got our closing statements coming up. We're going to put three minutes on the clock for each of you and, as is the tradition of these debates, we're going to do our closing statements in the opposite order of our opening remarks. So, Newt Gingrich, you are up first with your three-minute closing statement.

NEWT GINGRICH: Let me just suggest to you that, had they worded the proposal for the debate differently, it would have been impossible for us to have any arguments. If they had said that, to use your six-year-old's term, "Donald Trump's a 'pooh-pooh-head' and says really weird things sometimes," it would have been tough.

The objective reality is that this is the first person in American history never to have held any public office to come out of nowhere and defeat sixteen Republicans, defeat Hillary Clinton, defeat a billion-dollar campaign, defeat the elite media. He has done a hostile takeover of the Republican Party and a hostile takeover of the national government. And that kind of person probably has edges. Okay?

So, if the debate topic had been: "Be it resolved, Donald Trump has some edges and they are a little strange," I would have refused to come up here. I would have said, "Are you crazy?" I mean, I am willing to debate in front of Canadians, even if some of them boo, because I think you are so much better than, say, a Berkeley audience.

But still, you have got to have some sense here. That's not what the question is. America has many challenges. Venezuela has many challenges. Catalonia has many challenges. Austria has many challenges. Germany has many challenges. Britain has many challenges. We are living in a period where our culture and our economy are in turmoil. Where there are huge systems like Facebook and Google that are uncontrolled and that are changing the entire landscape, and all of us are having to adjust.

In that setting, the wording of the debate strikes me as almost impossible for them to carry. That the problems of the American democracy are Donald Trump? He's a manifestation of the problems. He was elected because a vast number of Americans are deeply uncomfortable. And they preferred taking the risk on somebody with rough edges, who would occasionally say rough things, because they thought he would at least break up the system that they thought was decaying and failing the country. And I think that's what's been happening.

Now, of course, if you are in the old order, or if you've grown up in the old order and you were part of the old order, this is all horrifying. And as I said at the beginning, I fully expect that, as the swamp diminishes, the alligators will be snapping and biting and arguing and yelling, "Autocrat, autocrat!" But, in fact, what's happening is that America is once again reinventing itself.

E. J. DIONNE: I want to thank you all for your attentiveness. And I have to say that I salute Newt Gingrich for trying to make Donald Trump seem almost cute and eccentric at the beginning of his talk. I also appreciate his calling us alligators, because they are cute in their own way.

I want to point out that what happened at the end of the debate is precisely what I said would happen, which is that our opponents here want to hang on a few words of this proposition and say that if you don't believe that Donald Trump caused all the problems that the United States faces, then you really can't vote for this proposition.

We are asserting something else. We are asserting that Donald Trump *is* the crisis, *is* the problem. They say that we presented no specifics. They couldn't really answer us on Joe Arpaio. They had to go off on a long bit of character assassination to dispute what we said about James Comey—which is true—which is that Donald Trump said that he didn't like what James Comey was doing about the Russian investigation. That should be genuinely alarming.

It is Trump who holds himself above the norms that every other politician, including Mr. Gingrich, hold themselves to. He says, "I don't have to get rid of my businesses.

I don't have to release my income tax returns. You don't have to know anything about me. I can do what I want." If that isn't autocratic, I don't know what is.

American democracy was never supposed to give us a leader like Donald Trump. We have had more or less ideological presidents, more or less competent presidents. We've had other presidents who have divided us, but never as consciously as Donald Trump has. We have never had a president who has aroused such grave and widespread doubts about his commitment to the institution of self-government and to the norms of democracy.

We urge you to vote for this proposition to send a message to us, meaning we Americans. I believe that the United States is more tolerant than Donald Trump. We are more committed to democratic freedoms than he is. The American people are more open to progress and hope and to the future. That is why the vast majority of Americans disapprove of Donald Trump.

Yes, Donald Trump has created the worst crisis for our democracy in generations. But I want to reassure all our Canadian friends here that we shall overcome.

KIMBERLEY STRASSEL: Let's think about what we have actually established here tonight. As Newt said, we have established that the president is a bit of a "pooh-pooh-head." He's a little odd, a little off. He definitely does not govern in a way that anyone else has. And he says things that many of us wish he wouldn't, all the time.

We have established that a lot of people do not agree with Donald Trump's policies, including Andrew and E. J., and are furious that he was elected, and will do what they can to discredit him in office. And that the media will do so, too. As Newt said, half of the stuff that comes out of the media is directly disputed by four-star generals and by others. But it doesn't stop them from writing it. So, there is an active and hostile campaign.

We've established that if you throw around lots of scary words like "autocrat," "tyranny," and "Putin," and put them in the same breath as "Donald Trump," that you can scare people and make them start thinking in an alternate reality from what's actually happening in Washington.

But here is what we have not established, because it goes to tonight's resolution. We have not established that Donald Trump has undermined or hurt in any way the actual rules and forms of democracy in the United States as we Americans view them.

They mentioned Jim Comey. The president had the right to fire him. They mentioned Joe Arpaio. He had the right to pardon him. They talk about different moves that he's taken. No one disputes that the president has the right to change regulations within health and human services, to change another president's health care law. You might not like how he's doing it. You might agree with the policy of before. And you might not like that he got rid of the climate program. But he did so because it was pushed through without congressional approval and had been immediately stayed by the Supreme Court because they recognized that it likely violated the Constitution because of the way it was put through.

Again, no one can point to anything that has undermined those basic structures.

AUDIENCE MEMBER: What about banning the LGBTQ from the military?

KIMBERLEY STRASSEL: I didn't know we were debating that. No one is disputing that he can do that, too. I am not saying it's the right policy.

AUDIENCE MEMBER: That's right.

KIMBERLEY STRASSEL: Many people can disagree, but you don't just get to revolt if you don't like it. This is why we have elections. And I appreciate that many people in this room did not like the way this election went. For many of us on the Republican side, Donald Trump was not our first choice for the nomination either. But we had an election that was peacefully conducted. It was honestly conducted. And there is no proof otherwise. And if you think so, you are reading that press again. Wait and see what actually happens before you make your mind up.

I ask you to vote against this. Don't believe the hype. Actually base this on the facts of what he's done so far.

ANDREW SULLIVAN: Ladies and gentlemen, I want to end in agreement with Speaker Gingrich that America and the world are facing extraordinary challenges—extraordinary challenges with the economy, with technology, and with the extraordinary dangers and difficulties of a multiracial and multicultural society.

America is the first white majority country in the history of the world to become a non-white majority country. Technology is ripping people's lives apart. It is impoverishing many people and stagnating the wages of many more. It is a difficult, emotional, troubling time.

But it's precisely because we're in such a difficult moment that it is vital that the Constitution of the United States, respect for the rule of law in the United States, civility in our language and discourse are maintained in the United States, and that rules and norms and procedures that have protected our democracy for centuries be upheld.

And that is why, when we have a president who has contempt for that Constitution, who has pushed it in nine months to the breaking point, who has exhibited every capacity and instinct for authoritarian rule, who delights in dividing, whose statements divide Americans every day in completely unnecessary ways, a man who can turn the National Football League into a matter of deep division, and who acts on the international stage with a recklessness and an ignorance and a pride and a vanity, that puts all of us and our lives and our security at stake.

It is because he is absolutely the worst possible answer to these problems that he is intensifying and deepening these divisions; that he is tearing America apart emotionally, culturally, and politically; that the country is fast dividing into two warring tribes. And the one person that we need at this moment to bridge those divides, to address these problems with sincerity, is the president. And he had a chance, if he had reached out to the Democrats. If he had engaged in infrastructure. If he had withheld his vicious tongue. If he were able to control himself, he could have been a great president. But he isn't.

He is what he is. And what he is, is a danger the likes of which we haven't seen in our lifetimes. Vote for this proposition.

RUDYARD GRIFFITHS: Thank you. That was a terrific and hard-fought debate. And it reminds me of something Peter Munk once said on this stage, which is that it's one thing to give a speech in front of an audience of people who agree or disagree with you, but something quite different to get on a stage and engage in verbal and mental combat with your intellectual peers.

So, ladies and gentlemen, a round of applause for our debaters. Fabulous debate.

Well, we are going to have some fun now. You've got a chance to vote again on tonight's resolution. We know what it is: "Be it resolved, American democracy is in the worst crisis in a generation and Donald J. Trump is to blame." Let's take a look again at how you voted at the start of tonight's debate: 33 percent of you disagreed. The rest of you were in favour of the motion.

And, again, we asked how many of you could change your minds. Upwards of 80 percent might potentially switch your vote to one side or the other. You each have a ballot in your program. There is a pencil with that ballot and there are ballot boxes on the way out. Vote once. Vote carefully. Send a message.

And, again, thank you, ladies and gentlemen, for being part of tonight's Munk Debate. We'll do it all again in the spring.

Summary: The pre-debate vote was 67 percent in favour of the resolution, 33 percent against it. The final vote showed 64 percent in favour of the motion and 36 percent against. Given that more of the voters shifted to the team against the resolution, the victory goes to Newt Gingrich and Kimberley Strassel.

Post-Debate Interviews with Moderator
Rudyard Griffiths

NEWT GINGRICH AND KIMBERLEY STRASSEL IN CONVERSATION WITH RUDYARD GRIFFITHS

RUDYARD GRIFFITHS: Thank you. That was a very heated debate. There were people giving you standing ovations at the end. We rarely have that happen.

NEWT GINGRICH: I think that Andrew Sullivan and E. J. Dionne are tremendous and did a great job, and I'm delighted that Kim came all the way from Alaska.

KIMBERLEY STRASSEL: Newt was my secret weapon today. We probably would have done better had I said nothing.

NEWT GINGRICH: No, you were great. And all of us ended up quoting your six-year-old.

RUDYARD GRIFFITHS: The new star of the debate. Kimberley, give us your high and low points of the debate, either on your team or the other side.

KIMBERLEY STRASSEL: For me, the high point of the day was listening to Newt talk about the media, which has played such a debilitating role in the way Donald Trump is viewed in America. And, I think, an intellectually dishonest one.

The low point of the debate was that obviously neither Newt nor I agree with every single thing that this president does, including the tone of some of the things he says. I don't think being asked to defend that was something that either of us necessarily came up on the stage to do.

RUDYARD GRIFFITHS: The same question for you, Newt. Favourite moment? Maybe something you left unsaid that you wish you'd said?

NEWT GINGRICH: My favourite moment was when Kim cited her six-year-old about "pooh-pooh-head," because it just captured the situation and it got us. This is my third debate here, and the thing I'll most remember is the degree to which E. J. and Andrew were so passionate that they almost couldn't contain themselves. We would poke at them and they would come lunging back into the debate. In that sense, this was far and away the most emotional of the debates that I have participated in.

RUDYARD GRIFFITHS: It was quite charged. Kimberley, any thoughts on how the vote will go? I thought the initial vote would be much more in favour of the motion, and that with an audience we might have 80 or 90 percent saying, "You know what? Trump is to blame." Were you surprised by that? And do you have any sense of which way this is going to go?

KIMBERLEY STRASSEL: Newt looked at me when you said that, and whispered, "This is not good for us." You want everyone to believe so that if you can just get a couple of people onto your side, you can pull it off. But I'm not sure if we will pull that off. The depth of feeling out there in the audience is very anti-Trump. And we were up against very good debaters on the other side.

NEWT GINGRICH: The one thing that surprised me—if we'd had the time I would have gone back to it and tried to draw the audience in—was when Kimberley said something that was factually true about Hillary. There was a section on the upper left who literally groaned, as though it was a topic you weren't allowed to discuss. I found it fascinating—the immediate spontaneity and the intensity of the reaction was very interesting. Last year, you will remember, when I came we had 14 percent voting for our side, and we got it up to 20, and everybody told me what a great victory it was. So, I'm a little worried that we started at 32 and we might end up at 14. But we'll see. It was a lot of fun.

I think that if they vote their sense about Trump, we're in trouble. But if they vote the actual question, the other side could have a very hard time. Bringing up examples like Arpaio, I think, actually hurt them. But we'll see.

RUDYARD GRIFFITHS: I want to thank you both. It's courageous to get out there, to debate people face to face. A credit to both of you for doing it.

NEWT GINGRICH: The Munk Debates are a great national institution. I'm so delighted you guys do it, and that Peter had the wisdom to set this up.

KIMBERLEY STRASSEL: This is one of the most fun things I have ever done. Thank you.

E. J. DIONNE AND ANDREW SULLIVAN
IN CONVERSATION WITH RUDYARD GRIFFITHS

RUDYARD GRIFFITHS: Thank you both. I'm really sincere about this: that is a difficult stage. You're in front of 3,000 people, the shots are coming in one after another, and you've got to keep your wits about you and send those zingers right back. You both did that tonight.

Andrew, to start with you, is there something you left unsaid tonight that you'd like to use this opportunity to bring up? Or is there something your opponents said that you want to come back to now?

ANDREW SULLIVAN: The one concession I want to make is that the Constitution *has* survived so far. It's been quite robust. The press have performed their duty and Congress has performed theirs. And while the courts have, in some cases, overreacted, that's a good thing, not a bad thing. But I'd stress again that this man has pushed the Constitution to the limit in just nine months, and that everything he says suggests a sort of impending violation of it.

Give us a major crisis. Give us a terror attack. Give us the launch of a war. And I am profoundly concerned about the man who will be in charge of us all, and whether he could even command the trust or belief that he must in such a situation. We are in some ways living on borrowed time. That's why I think he must be removed as soon as possible.

RUDYARD GRIFFITHS: E. J., was there maybe something left unsaid or an argument from the other side that you thought deserves a special post-debate rebuttal?

E. J. DIONNE: What bothered me is that no matter what Andrew and I said, Newt and Kim just replied, "Well, that doesn't count." Joe Arpaio is an actual act, and we think it really does count. That's a real thing. The firing of Comey is a real thing. I found it disturbing that I could see Speaker Gingrich building a case for firing Mueller by saying, "Well, there is something illegitimate about this whole investigation; they were all Hillary people." Paradoxically, that feeds right into our argument, because that is what we are worried about—that the president will use the appearance of partisanship as an excuse to undermine the rule of the law. We'll see what the audience made of this argument. But that disturbed me.

The other thing we probably could have spent more time on is Senator Corker's idea that there is something terribly wrong about a president whose aides feel they have to protect the country from him. We got into that a little, but I think it's a point we might have hammered home if we had had another five or ten minutes.

RUDYARD GRIFFITHS: Andrew, what did you think of the audience? They were really reacting. It was great to hear the catcalling, the booing, the applauding.

ANDREW SULLIVAN: It was. I did not expect a round of applause when I defended sovereignty, and then I realized, "Oh, it's because my three minutes are up." That was my only real shock. But they were great, apart from the heckling at the end. But, you know, a little heckling is fine. It was very Canadian.

E. J. DIONNE: And it was a heckle for a particular purpose because it was an issue that we had not raised. And he waited until the end and wanted to make sure that point got in.

ANDREW SULLIVAN: And that's a legitimate policy decision by a president. What isn't legitimate is to tell no one and to tweet it out as a fiat without going through the proper chain of command. Treating the lives of LGBTQ service members who are serving their country as if they are chaff in the wind, that you can manipulate and use—it's just not right.

E. J. DIONNE: It also underscores the point you made, and I was really grateful that you drove this home, which is that there are divisions in the country. A president can try to heal them or he can try to deepen them. And one of the most troubling things about Donald Trump is that he wants the divisions because they serve his political purposes. That's not an invented charge. You simply have to watch his behaviour on issue after issue. Why in the world are we having a national discussion about football players of the NFL kneeling? This is because it serves his political interests to divide us.

ANDREW SULLIVAN: I think that may even be overestimating him. I think he cannot help it. He is devoid of any ability to control his thoughts; he has no self-restraint, no controlling mechanism in his brain or in his gut. So, we have someone who can't control himself who is in control of us. That is terrifying.

RUDYARD GRIFFITHS: Finally, do you have a sense of how this vote could unfold? A lot of people were up for changing their mind—upwards of 80 percent. I thought that was interesting.

E. J. DIONNE: I was very curious how true that figure was. I guess, if you are attending a debate you at least want to say to the people on that stage, "I am willing to listen; I am open-minded."

But I don't really know how we played. I had a sense occasionally from the applause that we were gaining some ground. But there were a couple of moments where I thought they seemed to score points.

I'd like a lot more polling information about this audience because I think it depends which message they want to send, and it will be interesting to see what choice they make. I wish there were a second question, which is: "Why did you vote — on points in the debate, or did you decide you wanted to send a different message?"

RUDYARD GRIFFITHS: Andrew, your thoughts? I've done twenty of these debates and I usually come out with some sense of which way it's going to go. Tonight, I'm totally flummoxed. I don't know how this is going to work out.

ANDREW SULLIVAN: I don't know either. And, happily, I'm not responsible for anything anymore. So, whatever they want to say. For me, that's part of the game tonight. But in reality, this is really a lot more important than a game.

I'm really grateful for the opportunity to vent and to say what I believe about it. And I know Newt said it was like a Shakespearean actor, but I said nothing I don't believe in.

E. J. DIONNE: I think that was a high compliment, actually.

ANDREW SULLIVAN: Yes, I'm sure it was.

I do think they have a point. The Constitution has held up. But everybody says that until it doesn't.

E. J. DIONNE: The other odd thing is that being in Canada is like being almost no place else. It's like being at a cousin's house. It wouldn't be the same holding this debate in a lot of other countries that are friendly to the United States. Canada is like family to us. Now, it's literally true in my case. But I was thinking a lot about both the similarities and the differences between the United States and Canada within this closeness.

ANDREW SULLIVAN: If you look at the polling in America, 57 percent of Republicans say there is nothing that Donald Trump could do to change their mind about him. And around 56 percent of Democrats say the same thing. Here, it seemed that there are people, like most sane people in the world, who are alarmed by what's going on in Washington, but you didn't get the sense that we are in a tribal situation. You can't, for example, go to a university in our country without being surrounded by the Far Left, and the idea of having a dialogue there with anybody is impossible.

RUDYARD GRIFFITHS: Well, gentlemen, a well-deserved drink awaits you. Thank you again for coming here to do this.

E. J. DIONNE: Thank you.

ANDREW SULLIVAN: Thank you.

ACKNOWLEDGEMENTS

The Munk Debates are the product of the public-spiritedness of a remarkable group of civic-minded organizations and individuals. First and foremost, these debates would not be possible without the vision and leadership of the Aurea Foundation. Founded in 2006 by Peter and Melanie Munk, the Aurea Foundation supports Canadian individuals and institutions involved in the study and development of public policy. The debates are the foundation's signature initiative, a model for the kind of substantive public policy conversation Canadians can foster globally. Since the creation of the debates in 2008, the foundation has underwritten the entire cost of each semi-annual event. The debates have also benefited from the input and advice of members of the board of the foundation, including Mark Cameron, Andrew Coyne, Devon Cross, Allan Gotlieb, Margaret MacMillan, Anthony Munk, Robert Prichard, and Janice Stein.

For her contribution to the preliminary edit of the book, the debate organizers would like to thank Jane McWhinney.

Since their inception, the Munk Debates have sought to take the discussions that happen at each event to national and international audiences. Here the debates have benefited immeasurably from a partnership with Canada's national newspaper, the *Globe and Mail*, and the counsel of its editor-in-chief, David Walmsley.

With the publication of this superb book, House of Anansi Press is helping the debates reach new audiences in Canada and around the world. The debates' organizers would like to thank Anansi chair Scott Griffin and president and publisher Sarah MacLachlan for their enthusiasm for this book project and insights into how to translate the spoken debate into a powerful written intellectual exchange.

ABOUT THE DEBATERS

E. J. DIONNE JR. is a senior fellow at the Brookings Institution, a syndicated columnist for the *Washington Post*, and professor in the foundations of democracy and culture at Georgetown University. A frequent commentator on American politics for National Public Radio, ABC's "This Week," and MSNBC, he is the author of the recent bestseller *Why the Right Went Wrong: Conservatism from Goldwater to the Tea Party and Beyond*. His new book is *One Nation After Trump*.

ANDREW SULLIVAN is a conservative political commentator, a former editor of the *New Republic*, and the author or editor of six books. He is a contributing editor at *New York Magazine*, where he writes about American politics and culture. Prior to joining *New York Magazine*, he was a contributor at the *Atlantic Monthly* and the *Daily Beast*. The *New York Times* said of his commentary, "Sullivan might deserve to be remembered as the most influential political writer of his generation."

NEWT GINGRICH is a former Speaker of the United States House of Representatives, *New York Times* bestselling author, and *Time* magazine Man of the Year. Called "the indispensable leader" by the *Washington Times*, he was the architect of the Contract with America, which saw the Republican Party capture a majority in the U.S. House of Representatives for the first time in forty years. The author of eighteen books of nonfiction, Speaker Gingrich's latest is *Understanding Trump.*

KIMBERLEY STRASSEL is a journalist, author, and political commentator. She writes the influential "Potomac Watch" column for the *Wall Street Journal*, and serves on the paper's editorial board. A frequent political commentator on U.S. television, she moderated the high-stakes South Carolina Republican presidential debate. In 2014, she received the Bradley Prize for journalistic excellence, which provides "important analyses on issues of the day [strengthening] the American fabric."

ABOUT THE EDITOR

RUDYARD GRIFFITHS is the chair of the Munk Debates and president of the Aurea Charitable Foundation. He is the editor of thirteen books on history, politics, and international affairs, including *Who We Are: A Citizen's Manifesto*, which was a *Globe and Mail* Best Book of 2009 and a finalist for the Shaughnessy Cohen Prize for Political Writing. He lives in Toronto with his wife and two children.

ABOUT THE MUNK DEBATES

The Munk Debates are Canada's premier public policy event. Held semi-annually, the debates provide leading thinkers with a global forum to discuss the major public policy issues facing the world and Canada. Each event takes place in Toronto in front of a live audience, and the proceedings are covered by domestic and international media. Participants in recent Munk Debates include Anne Applebaum, Louise Arbour, Robert Bell, Tony Blair, John Bolton, Ian Bremmer, Stephen F. Cohen, Daniel Cohn-Bendit, Paul Collier, Howard Dean, Alain de Botton, Hernando de Soto, Alan Dershowitz, E. J. Dionne, Maureen Dowd, Gareth Evans, Nigel Farage, Mia Farrow, Niall Ferguson, William Frist, Newt Gingrich, Malcolm Gladwell, Jennifer Granholm, David Gratzer, Glenn Greenwald, Stephen Harper, Michael Hayden, Rick Hillier, Christopher Hitchens, Richard Holbrooke, Laura Ingraham, Josef Joffe, Robert Kagan, Garry Kasparov,

Henry Kissinger, Charles Krauthammer, Paul Krugman, Arthur B. Laffer, Lord Nigel Lawson, Stephen Lewis, David Daokui Li, Bjørn Lomborg, Lord Peter Mandelson, Elizabeth May, George Monbiot, Caitlin Moran, Dambisa Moyo, Thomas Mulcair, Vali Nasr, Alexis Ohanian, Camille Paglia, George Papandreou, Steven Pinker, Samantha Power, Vladimir Pozner, Robert Reich, Matt Ridley, David Rosenberg, Hanna Rosin, Simon Schama, Anne-Marie Slaughter, Bret Stephens, Mark Steyn, Kimberley Strassel, Andrew Sullivan, Lawrence Summers, Justin Trudeau, Amos Yadlin, and Fareed Zakaria.

The Munk Debates are a project of the Aurea Foundation, a charitable organization established in 2006 by philanthropists Peter and Melanie Munk to promote public policy research and discussion. For more information, visit www.munkdebates.com.

ABOUT THE INTERVIEWS

Rudyard Griffith's interviews with Newt Gingrich, Kimberley Strassel, E. J. Dionne, and Andrew Sullivan were recorded on October 12, 2017. The Aurea Foundation is gratefully acknowledged for permission to reprint excerpts from the following:

(p. 3) "Newt Gingrich in Conversation," by Rudyard Griffiths. Copyright © 2018 Aurea Foundation. Transcribed by Transcript Heroes.

(p. 11) "Kimberley Strassel in Conversation," by Rudyard Griffiths. Copyright © 2018 Aurea Foundation. Transcribed by Transcript Heroes.

(p. 19) "E. J. Dionne in Conversation," by Rudyard Griffiths. Copyright © 2018 Aurea Foundation. Transcribed by Transcript Heroes.

Is This the End of the Liberal International Order?
Niall Ferguson vs. Fareed Zakaria

Since the end of World War II, global affairs have been shaped by the increasing free movement of people and goods, international rules setting, and a broad appreciation of the mutual benefits of a more interdependent world. Together these factors defined the liberal international order and sustained an era of rising global prosperity and declining international conflict. But now, for the first time in a generation, the pillars of liberal internationalism are being shaken to their core by the reassertion of national borders, national interests, and nationalist politics across the globe. Can liberal internationalism survive these challenges and remain the defining rules-based system of the future? Or are we witnessing the beginning of the end of the liberal international order?

"We can no longer confidently talk about a liberal international order. It's become disorder in the sense that democracy has been disrupted." — *Niall Ferguson*

The Global Refugee Crisis: How Should We Respond?
Arbour and Schama vs. Farage and Steyn

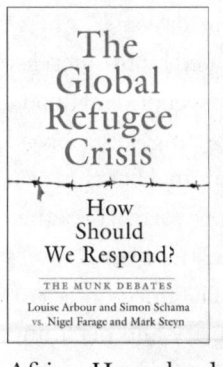

The world is facing the worst humanitarian crisis since the Second World War. Over 300,000 are dead in Syria, and one and a half million are either injured or disabled. Four and a half million people are trying to flee the country. And Syria is just one of a growing number of failed or failing states in the Middle East and North Africa. How should developed nations respond to human suffering on this mass scale? Do the prosperous societies of the West, including Canada and the United States, have a moral imperative to assist as many refugees as they reasonably and responsibly can? Or is this a time for vigilance and restraint in the face of a wave of mass migration that risks upending the tolerance and openness of the West?

"There's nothing to be ashamed of about having an emotional response to the suffering of four million Syrian refugees."
—Simon Schama

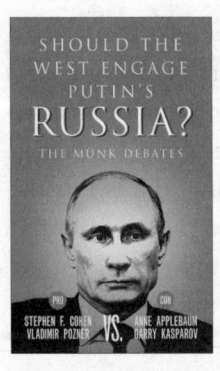

Has Obama Made the World a More Dangerous Place?
Kagan and Stephens vs. Zakaria and Slaughter

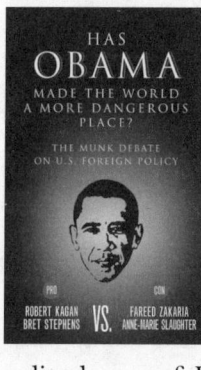

From Ukraine to the Middle East to China, the United States is redefining its role in international affairs. Famed historian and foreign policy commentator Robert Kagan and Pulitzer Prize–winning journalist Bret Stephens take on CNN's Fareed Zakaria and noted academic and political commentator Anne-Marie Slaughter to debate the foreign policy legacy of President Obama.

"Superpowers don't get to retire... In the international sphere, Americans have had to act as judge, jury, police, and, in the case of military action, executioner." —Robert Kagan

Are Men Obsolete?
Rosin and Dowd vs. Moran and Paglia

For the first time in history, will it be better to be a woman than a man in the upcoming century? Renowned author and editor Hanna Rosin and Pulitzer Prize–winning columnist Maureen Dowd challenge *New York Times*–bestselling author Caitlin Moran and trailblazing social critic Camille Paglia to debate the relative decline of the power and status of men in the workplace, the family, and society at large.

"Feminism was always wrong to pretend women could 'have it all.' It is not male society but Mother Nature who lays the heaviest burden on women." — *Camille Paglia*

North America's Lost Decade?

Krugman and Rosenberg vs. Summers and Bremmer

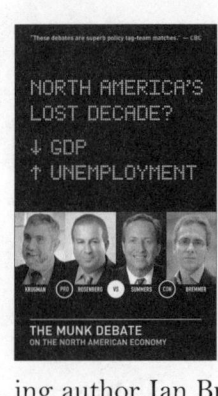

The future of the North American economy is more uncertain than ever. In this edition of the Munk Debates, Nobel Prize–winning economist Paul Krugman and chief economist and strategist at Gluskin Sheff + Associates David Rosenberg square off against former U.S. treasury secretary Lawrence Summers and bestselling author Ian Bremmer to tackle the resolution, "Be it resolved: North America faces a Japan-style era of high unemployment and slow growth."

"It's now impossible to deny the obvious, which is that we are not now, and have never been, on the road to recovery." — *Paul Krugman*

Hitchens vs. Blair
Christopher Hitchens vs. Tony Blair

Intellectual juggernaut and staunch atheist Christopher Hitchens goes head-to-head with former British prime minister Tony Blair, one of the Western world's most openly devout political leaders, on the age-old question: Is religion a force for good in the world? Few world leaders have had a greater hand in shaping current events than Blair; few writers have been more outspoken and polarizing than Hitchens.

Sharp, provocative, and thoroughly engrossing, *Hitchens vs. Blair* is a rigorous and electrifying intellectual sparring match on the contentious questions that continue to dog the topic of religion in our globalized world.

"If religious instruction were not allowed until the child had attained the age of reason, we would be living in a very different world." —Christopher Hitchens

The Munk Debates: Volume One
Edited by Rudyard Griffiths
Introduction by Peter Munk

Launched in 2008 by philanthropists Peter and Melanie Munk, the Munk Debates is Canada's premier international debate series, a highly anticipated cultural event that brings together the world's brightest minds.

This volume includes the first five debates in the series and features twenty leading thinkers and doers arguing for or against provocative resolutions that address pressing public policy concerns such as the future of global security, the implications of humanitarian intervention, the effectiveness of foreign aid, the threat of climate change, and the state of health care in Canada and the United States.

"By trying to highlight the most important issues at crucial moments in the global conversation, these debates not only profile the ideas and solutions of some of our brightest thinkers and doers, but crystallize public passion and knowledge, helping to tackle some global challenges confronting humankind."
— Peter Munk

houseofanansi.com/collections/munk-debates